North Korea

North Korea

BY PATRICIA K. KUMMER

Enchantment of the World™
Second Series

Children's Press®

An Imprint of Scholastic Inc.

NEW YORK   TORONTO   LONDON   AUCKLAND   SYDNEY
MEXICO CITY   NEW DELHI   HONG KONG
DANBURY, CONNECTICUT

Frontispiece: A farm near Wonsan, North Korea

Consultant: Dr. Tatiana Gabroussenko, Centre for Korean Studies of the Australian National University, Canberra, Australia

Please note: All statistics are as up-to-date as possible at the time of publication.

Book production by Herman Adler

Library of Congress Cataloging-in-Publication Data

Kummer, Patricia K.
 North Korea / by Patricia K. Kummer.
    p. cm.—(Enchantment of the world. Second series)
 Includes bibliographical references and index.
 ISBN-13: 978-0-531-18485-1
 ISBN-10: 0-531-18485-4
 1. Korea (North)—Juvenile literature. 2. Korea (North) I. Title.
 DS932.K78 2008
 951.93—dc22   2007025693

Acknowledgments

I wish to extend my thanks to the staff of the Lisle Library District for quickly obtaining research materials for me through interlibrary loan.

Contents

Cover photo:
Young North
Korean boy

North Korean children

Celadon pottery

Living in the Hermit Kingdom

SIX THOUSAND GIRLS ENTERED PYONGYANG INDOOR Stadium in the capital city of North Korea. They were dressed identically in white and blue leotards. Each carried a red ball. The conductor signaled the orchestra to play, and the girls began performing gymnastic routines.

For several hours every day for more than six months, groups of a few hundred girls had practiced these routines. They trained outdoors on unpadded concrete, enduring sub-freezing temperatures. Their goal was to perform the routines perfectly—each girl making the same move at the same exact time. Now the girls had achieved their goal: they were taking part in the Mass Games.

Everything about the Mass Games is on a huge scale. They take place in one of the world's largest stadiums, which seats 150,000 people. They make up the largest choreographed spectacle in the world. About 100,000 children, teenagers, young women, and soldiers perform in the games over several hours. Acts include gymnastic routines using

Opposite: **North Koreans in traditional dress attend an event in Kim Il Sung Square in Pyongyang.**

Young athletes perform at the Mass Games in 2007.

balls, jump ropes, and hoops; ballet movements; young couples dancing on roller skates; tumblers; baton twirlers; and soldiers doing taekwondo. Another 12,000 schoolchildren sit opposite the spectators in the "card" section. They each hold a book of large colored cards that they flip in unison to form scenes from North Korean history or portraits of their leader, Kim Jong Il, and his father, Kim Il Sung.

The Mass Games are officially held to honor Kim Jong Il, the ruler of North Korea. But for the thousands of young people taking part, the games have many other meanings. The games will help the gymnast on top of a pyramid become a star. They will help the lead tumbler get into the best college. They will make parents proud.

Thousands of North Koreans hold cards aloft to form a picture of Kim Il Sung at the Mass Games in 2007. The Mass Games is the largest choreographed event in the world.

North Korea began holding the Mass Games in 1946. Today, the games are a long-standing tradition, an essential part of North Korean life. In some ways, they have become a symbol of North Korea.

South Korean soldiers watch a train pass through a gate into the DMZ on May 17, 2007. It was one of the first two trains to cross the DMZ since the Korean War.

A Divided Peninsula

North Korea lies on the northern half of the Korean Peninsula. This peninsula is connected to China and juts out toward Japan in the waters off eastern Asia. The official name of North Korea is the Democratic People's Republic of Korea (DPRK). It is referred to as North Korea to distinguish it from the Korean Peninsula's other country—the Republic of Korea (ROK). The ROK is called South Korea by the rest of the world.

Since World War II ended in 1945, the Korean Peninsula has been divided almost in half. In 1948, the DPRK and the ROK officially set up their own governments. The two countries battled each other during the Korean War (1950–1953). At the end of that war, a Demilitarized Zone (DMZ) was created. The DMZ is a strip of land about 2.5 miles (4 kilometers) wide between the two countries, keeping them separate. The border is closed. This means that people cannot travel back and forth between the two countries freely.

What Is Korea?

In this book, the term *Korea* refers to the Korean Peninsula and to the nation or colony of Korea before 1945. The peninsula was divided in 1945, and two independent countries were established in 1948. In this book, we refer to the Democratic People's Republic of Korea (DPRK) as North Korea, and the Republic of Korea (ROK) as South Korea.

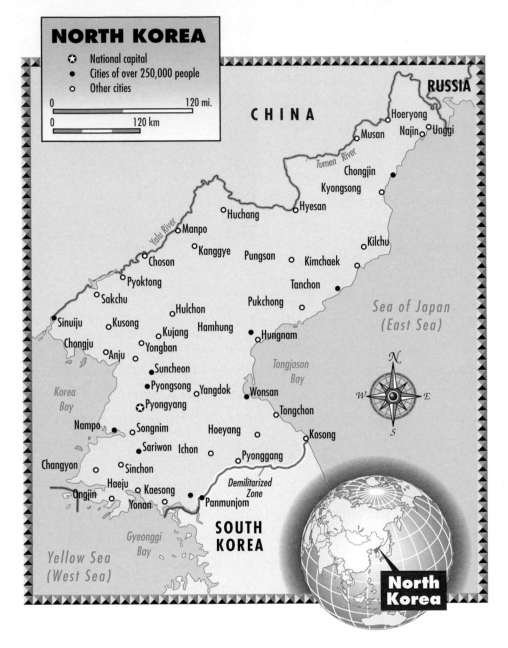

NORTH KOREA

- ✪ National capital
- ● Cities of over 250,000 people
- ○ Other cities

0 ——— 120 mi.

0 ——— 120 km

Since the end of the Korean War, the two Koreas have gone down different roads. North Korea has maintained a communist government. It has had only two leaders in its history—Kim Il Sung and his son, Kim Jong Il. Kim Jong Il is a dictator. He runs the country without letting the people have a real voice in the government. South Korea also suffered through a string of dictators. But since the late 1980s, it has become much more democratic and now has many political parties. North Korea's economy is controlled by the government and is very troubled. South Korea, meanwhile, is economically healthy. North Korea has little trade with other countries, while South Korea's economy depends on international trade.

Kim Jong Il keeps himself and his country isolated from the rest of the world. He seldom talks to other world leaders.

Despite the many differences between the two Koreas, the governments of both countries have talked about reunification. Little progress has been made, however. Many Koreans think it might be better to bring the people of Korea back together, instead of the governments. If the border was opened, families that were split apart when Korea was divided could be reunited. Trade and tourism between the two countries could also increase. Since 2000, some of these activities have occurred. A few highways and rail lines now connect the two countries, but they are not open for private

A Note on Spelling

The two Koreas do not spell all words in the same way. In 2000, the South Korean government changed the way words are spelled when using the Latin alphabet. That's the alphabet of English. For example, Mount *Paektu* is now written as Mount *Baekdu*, and the city name *Kaesong* is spelled *Gaeseong*. North Korea continues to use the older spellings, and those spellings are used in this book.

use. Some South Koreans have been allowed to travel to North Korea for reunions with family members or as tourists to limited areas. North Koreans do not have the freedom to travel south, however.

Nicknames Tell a Story

During their five-thousand-year history, the Korean people have had a variety of names for their land. Perhaps the best-known name is Choson, which means "Land of the Morning Calm." Koreans say that this name comes from the peaceful way the land looks in the morning. At that time of day, mist hangs over the mountains, creating a dreamlike effect. Because mountains cover

A misty day at Mount Paektu, the highest mountain in North Korea. Paektu is the legendary birthplace of the Korean people.

North Korean kindergartners eat a meal.

most of the Korean Peninsula, "Land of the Morning Calm" is a name that applies to the entire peninsula.

The Korean Peninsula has experienced many events that could hardly be called calm. Over the centuries, armies from China, Mongolia, Manchuria, and Japan have marched onto the peninsula and tried to conquer the Korean people. After pushing back an invasion in the 1640s, Korea's rulers closed the country to contact with the outside world. Until Korea was forced to open up in 1876, the country was known as "the Hermit Kingdom."

Even during hard times, the Korean people maintained their spirit and held onto their culture. This is shown today in the ethnic background of the people in North Korea. They are almost entirely of Korean heritage. In fact, the government forbids intermarriage with people from other countries. Koreans have also continued to speak their own language, play their traditional music, and cook their traditional foods.

The Korean people were also sometimes known among their neighbors as "the Courteous People of the East." This name came from the courteous way Koreans treated one another and, particularly, the way they treated foreigners. Koreans followed a strict social code of conduct. Because of this code, everyone knew exactly what was expected and where

A statue of Kim Il Sung dominates a square in Pyongyang. The statue, which was built in 1972, is 66 feet (20 m) tall.

they stood in relationship to everyone else. Although life is difficult for North Koreans, they still extend courtesy and respect to one another and to the few foreign visitors to their country.

North Korea Today

Many Western visitors refer to North Korea today as "Kimland." That is because Kim Jong Il, who in North Korea is officially called "Dear Leader," and his father, Kim Il Sung, who is called "Great Leader," have woven their personalities into North Korea's government, economy, and society. In fact, after the elder Kim's death, North Korea's constitution was renamed the Kim Il Sung Constitution. Shrines to and portraits of the two men are common throughout North Korea. North Koreans are supposed to look upon them as godlike figures. According to the government, North Koreans live, work, and compete in sports to honor their leaders. They must bow down to pictures, posters, and statues of the leaders and thank them for all that they have. Because the North Korean people are kept isolated from the rest of the world, it is hard to know what they really think of the Kims.

The Kims have a philosophy called *juche*, which promotes the idea that North Korea is self-reliant. It can take care of itself and defend itself. Because of juche, North Koreans have been cut off from people in other countries. The government censors all the news they receive. Only high-level government officials have access to the Internet.

Similarly, the North Korean government limits what news about the country actually reaches the outside world. Outsiders know little about life in North Korea. Even when foreigners are allowed to visit, they can only see certain places. For these reasons, North Korea is sometimes still called by its old nickname, the Hermit Kingdom.

In 2002, U.S. president George W. Bush said North Korea was part of an "axis of evil." The label was applied because North Korea could possibly make nuclear, biological, and chemical weapons. In the years since, North Korea has continued to develop and test weapons that threaten South Korea and other nations. It has also sometimes said that it will stop developing nuclear weapons and allow weapons inspectors into the country. Will talks between North and South Korea, the United States, and other nations help calm the tensions and make the region safer? Only time will tell.

A high school student works on a computer. Computers have become increasingly common in North Korea.

Half a Peninsula

Jagged mountains tower over much of North Korea.

NORTH KOREA OCCUPIES THE NORTHERN HALF OF THE Korean Peninsula, in eastern Asia. To the north is China and a sliver of Russia. To the south, across the Demilitarized Zone (DMZ), lies South Korea. North Korea's other borders are water. To the west, the Yellow Sea, which Koreans call the West Sea, separates the Korean Peninsula from part of eastern China. To the east is the Sea of Japan, which Koreans call the East Sea. North Korea covers 46,609 square miles (120,717 sq km), which makes it a little smaller than the state of Mississippi.

Opposite: **A watchtower rises along the edge of the Demilitarized Zone.**

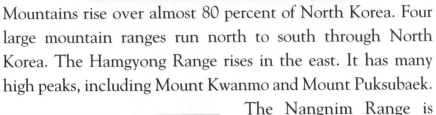

A Mountainous Land

Mountains rise over almost 80 percent of North Korea. Four large mountain ranges run north to south through North Korea. The Hamgyong Range rises in the east. It has many high peaks, including Mount Kwanmo and Mount Puksubaek.

Mount Kumgang is famous for its lush forests and steep ravines.

The Nangnim Range is farther to the west, while the Myohyang Range lies to the southwest. In this range is Mount Myohyang, which has become a shrine to Kim Il Sung and a tourist destination. Far to the west, near the Chinese border, is the Kangnam Range.

The Taebaek Range runs along North Korea's southeastern coast and extends into South Korea. These mountains drop steeply into the Sea of Japan. Mount Kumgang, the highest peak in this range, is also known as Diamond Mountain. It is famous for its beauty and has become popular among foreign tourists.

Mount Paektu, the highest point on the Korean Peninsula, rises along the North Korea–China border. It is an extinct volcanic mountain. Cheonji Lake has formed in the volcano's crater. From Mount Paektu, the Yalu River flows west into the Yellow Sea, forming part of North Korea's border with China. The Tumen River flows east from Mount Paektu. It forms the rest of the border with China and the border with Russia, before emptying into the Sea of Japan.

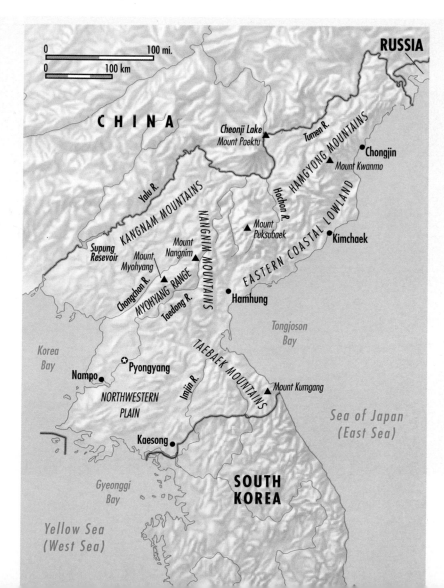

North Korea's Geographic Features

Area: 46,609 square miles (120,717 sq km)

Highest Elevation: 9,003 feet (2,744 m) above sea level, Mount Paektu

Lowest Elevation: Sea level, along the coasts

Longest River: Yalu River, 501 miles (806 km) long

Largest Lake: Cheonji Lake, 8.7 miles (14 km) around, 1,260 feet (384 m) deep

Longest Shared Border: 880 miles (1,416 km), with China

Coastline: 1,550 miles (2,495 km)

Greatest Distance North to South: 370 miles (595 km)

Greatest Distance East to West: 320 miles (515 km)

The other 20 percent of North Korea's land is lowlands, plains, and low hills. Several long rivers and many short, fast-running streams flow from the mountains across the plains. A narrow strip of lowlands lies along the Sea of Japan. The fish in these coastal waters provide an important source of protein for North Koreans. Inland from the coast are plains separated by low hills that make up most of the region. This is an important agricultural region. Some of North Korea's largest cities, including Chongjin, Hamhung, and Kimchaek, are also found in this area.

A North Korean fisherman repairs his net. Fishing is common in the nation's rivers and along the coasts.

A Look at North Korea's Cities

The capital city of Pyongyang is by far the largest city in North Korea. Nampo is the second-largest city. Located at the mouth of the Taedong River, about 30 miles (50 km) southwest of Pyongyang, it is the country's major western port. The city's main industries are shipbuilding, glassmaking, and gold and copper refining.

Hamhung, on the eastern coast, is North Korea's third-largest city. Founded as a government center during the Choson dynasty, Hamhung is now a major port. Best known for its hydroelectric power plant, Hamhung is also the center of North Korea's chemical industry.

Far to the north along the eastern coast lies Chongjin (above), North Korea's fourth-largest city. Once a small fishing village, Chongjin is now North Korea's main northeastern seaport and an important industrial city. The city is home to many steel and textile mills as well as factories that make rubber and railroad equipment. Coal-mining equipment is also produced in Chongjin, and large coal mines are nearby. Chongjin is not near a farming region, so it was hit hard when famine struck North Korea in the 1990s.

In the far southwestern corner of North Korea just north of the DMZ sits Kaesong (left). Kaesong was once the capital of the Koryo dynasty. Today, it is North Korea's fifth-largest city. The tomb of King Kongmin of the Koryo dynasty is on a hill above the city. The Koryo Museum exhibits traditional pottery and Buddhist relics. North of the city, Pakyon Falls provides a quiet area for hiking. Also outside of the city is the Kaesong Industrial Region, a complex of South Korean factories that employ North Koreans.

The Tumen River marks part of the border between North Korea and China. In winter, it is usually frozen over.

Another plain lies along North Korea's western coast. It has North Korea's best farmland. North Korea's capital city, Pyongyang, sits on the Taedong River in this region. Several other large industrial cities have also developed in the northwest, including Nampo and Kaesong. About half of North Korea's population lives in this region.

Climate

In many ways, North Korea's climate is like that of the Upper Midwest of the United States. It has cold winters and hot, humid summers. Winter starts in early December and ends in late March. Throughout winter, cold winds blow down the peninsula from northern Asia. Winter also brings heavy snowfall, especially in the mountains.

In early spring, yellow dust and sand blow down from deserts in China. By mid-April, North Korea begins to warm up. Farmers plant seeds and prepare rice fields. Summer is North Korea's wettest season. Winds called monsoons draw warm, wet air from the southeast Pacific Ocean over Korea. The heaviest rains fall in the south, while all over the country it is hot and sticky.

Most North Koreans agree that fall is the best season. By then, the heavy summer rains have ended, temperatures have cooled a bit, and the air is dryer. Crops are harvested, and the landscape turns from shades of green to brilliant yellows, oranges, and reds as the leaves change color.

North Korean farmers first plant rice seeds in beds. In May, they transplant the young seedlings to fields.

The Natural Environment

KOREA HAS A LONG TRADITION OF PROTECTING THE environment. Conservation laws were passed as early as the A.D. 500s. For centuries, monks guarded the natural areas around their monasteries. Today, many of North Korea's national parks are on the sites of ancient monasteries. North Korea has more than thirty protected areas, including national parks and reserves. Its oldest and largest trees are found in these protected areas, as are most of the country's wild animals.

Opposite: **The baikal teal is one of twenty-five duck species found in North Korea.**

Students plant trees at Mount Kumgang National Park.

North Korea's National Parks

Because North Korea is a mountainous land, most of its protected areas are near peaks. Mount Paektu Biosphere Reserve sits on the border with China. Highlights of the reserve include the highest peak on the entire Korean Peninsula; Lake Cheonji, which is one of the world's deepest mountain lakes; and large areas of forest that have never been cut.

Mount Myohyang National Park is in southwestern North Korea. The park is most famous for the Pyohon Temple Complex, one of the most important Zen monasteries in Korea, which dates back to A.D. 1044. The park also features Ryongmun Big Cave, which extends for 4 miles (7 km) under the ground. The International Friendship Exhibition (right), a massive treasure house of gifts given to North Korea's leaders over the years, is found deep in the park's forests.

Mount Kumgang (above) rests in the southeastern corner of North Korea. This granite mountain is also known as Diamond Mountain because it sparkles like diamonds. The park is famed for its many stone pillars and other formations. Ponds, waterfalls, and deep ravines also grace the mountain. Several Buddhist temples and monks' living quarters on the mountain have been restored.

For the most part, nature in North Korea's national parks is protected and left unchanged. The natural environment in much of the rest of the country has not fared so well. Much of North Korea's cities are covered with concrete—wide streets, huge monuments, and multistory hotels and apartment buildings. The only green areas in cities are grassy parks along rivers where people can picnic and play games. In the countryside, most plains and hills no longer have trees.

Most of North Korea's forests had been cut down by 1950. The wood was used for cooking and as heating fuel. Other trees were cut for lumber or to clear farmland. During the 1990s, a terrible famine struck North Korea. Hungry people stripped trees of their bark and leaves. They were used as ingredients in watery broths.

The government has established programs to renew the forests, and many pine and scrub oak trees have been planted. But most hills remain barren despite these efforts. Some North Koreans who fled to South Korea were surprised by the large amounts of greenery there.

A woman pulls a cart past flowering trees near Pyongyang.

Forests and Flowers

About 4,000 kinds of plants grow in North Korea, including about 160 kinds of trees native to Korea. The most densely forested areas that remain are in the mountains. Many kinds of pine trees, such as spruce, larch, cedar, and Siberian fir, grow on the mountain slopes. Pine trees have long been important in Korean art and folklore. They are admired for their color, form, and fragrance. Pine leaves and nuts are the main source of food for many birds and wild animals.

Flowers for the Leaders

North Korea's leaders have had special flowers bred in their honor. The *kimilsungia* is an orchid developed by an Indonesian plant expert and presented to Kim Il Sung in 1965. In 1988, a Japanese plant expert presented a red begonia called the *kimjongilia* to Kim Jong Il. In 2006, the festival celebrating Kim Jong Il's birthday featured more than 23,000 kimjongilias (right). The Central Botanical Garden in Pyongyang includes special hothouses for these two flower breeds.

Willow and birch are also important trees in Korea. To Koreans, the willow symbolizes peace and beauty. Pyongyang has been called the Capital of Willows. A row of willow trees was planted there in about 1122 B.C. Today, willow trees line the city's parks along the Taedong River. The birch tree, called the *pakdal*, is also symbolic in North Korea. The legendary founder of Korea, Tangun, was born under a pakdal tree on Mount Paektu. Birch is one of the hardest woods available in North Korea, and it is sometimes used to make tool handles. Other hardwood trees found in North Korea's mountains include beech, elm, and gingko.

An important plant in North Korea is ginseng. Its roots are believed to improve strength and health. North Koreans use it in foods, drinks, and medicines. Although ginseng root is now grown commercially, the most powerful roots still grow in the wild.

Many kinds of flowering plants bloom in North Korea. Azaleas, gentians, and rhododendrons grow in the mountains. Cosmos, chrysanthemums, dianthuses, fuchsias, and lilies bloom at lower elevations. Lotus blossoms are found in ponds.

The National Flower

In 1991, Kim Il Sung named a hardy variety of magnolia North Korea's national flower. Kim said that the Korean people welcomed his army with this white flower as it marched into the peninsula after World War II. Because the magnolia is a strong flower, it is said to represent the spirit of the Korean people.

The Siberian tiger is extremely rare. Worldwide, only about five hundred live in the wild.

Wildlife

The damage to North Korea's forests has destroyed the habitats of many animals. At one time, antelope, bears, leopards, lynx, and Siberian tigers roamed North Korea's forests and mountains. Although most scientists believe the great cats no longer live in North Korea, the tiger and the lynx might still survive near Mount Paektu. In recent years, a few bears have been spotted there as well.

Today, the largest animals found in North Korea in any great numbers are wild boars and deer. Some wolves also live in the forests. Smaller animals in North Korea include badgers, foxes, martens, northern pikas, water shrews, muskrats, and Manchurian weasels. The Amur goral, an antelope with small, cone-shaped horns, is now endangered.

Bird-watchers have recorded more than three hundred kinds of birds in North Korea. Only a few of these birds are native to the country. Most of them just pass through. The endangered Tristram's woodpecker is found in southwestern North Korea. Herons, cranes, and other waterbirds nest in the wetlands along the Tumen River and in rice paddies. Many other birds, such as black grouse, hawk owls, rufous-backed buntings, and several kinds of woodpeckers, find homes in trees on Mount Paektu.

North Korea's waters are home to many other animals. Carp and eels live in the rivers. Sharks, squid, and octopuses are among the many large creatures found off the coasts. More common are shellfish such as abalones, clams, oysters, scallops, and shrimps. Pollack, filefish, and sardines are a few of the other fish found along the coast.

An Unplanned Nature Reserve

Perhaps the only good thing to come from the Korean War is the nature reserve that developed in the Demilitarized Zone (DMZ). Since 1953, barbed wire has enclosed this stretch of land, keeping people out. As a result, the DMZ became a haven for rare animals.

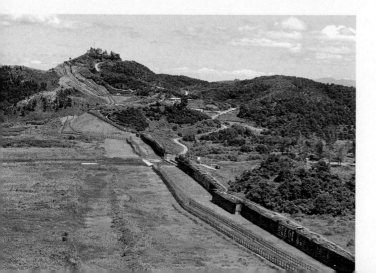

Amur leopards, Asiatic black bears, Eurasian lynx, and Amur gorals live in the DMZ. Some scientists think they have found footprints of Siberian tigers. Migratory birds such as black-faced spoonbills, red-crowned cranes, and white-naped cranes spend the winter in the DMZ. Nearly three thousand kinds of plants have also sprung up there.

In recent years, North Korea and South Korea have started trade and tourism programs. Two railroad lines and two highways now cross the DMZ, though they are little used. Environmentalists fear that more development in the DMZ will threaten the area's rare plant and animal life.

Five Thousand Years of History

This Korean egg cup dates back to the 1100s.

Ｐ EOPLE WERE LIVING ON THE KOREAN PENINSULA AS EARLY as 28,000 B.C. Tools and pottery from these early people have been found near the present-day cities of Pyongyang in North Korea and Seoul and Pusan in South Korea. In about 3000 B.C., people moved from the Altai Mountains of central Asia onto the Korean Peninsula. They likely pushed the earlier people off the peninsula. Modern Koreans trace their ancestry and their spoken language to these central Asian migrants. For this reason, Koreans say their history spans five thousand years.

Opposite: **Japanese soldiers storming a gate in Pyongyang in 1894**

Tangun: The Legendary Founder of Korea

According to legend, Tangun is the founder of Korea and the father of the Korean people. His father was Hwanung, the son of the ruler of heaven. His mother was a woman who had been a bear until Hwanung transformed her. The legend says that Tangun was born near Mount Paektu under a birch tree. In 2333 B.C., Tangun is said to have moved to Pyongyang, where he built a walled city and established the Ancient Choson Kingdom. Tangun is supposed to have lived more than a thousand years before he became a mountain god in far northern Korea. Today, Koreans celebrate October 3 as National Foundation Day. On that day in 2333 B.C., Tangun supposedly founded Ancient Choson.

This Korean Buddhist painting was made in 1755. Buddhism reached the Korean Peninsula in the 300s.

Ancient Choson and Chinese Influence

The early Koreans hunted, fished, and gathered food. Later, they began to farm. In time, they founded the Ancient Choson Kingdom. Ancient Choson was probably located between the Liao River in southern Manchuria, in what is now China, and the Taedong River in what is now North Korea. Large clans built walled towns in Ancient Choson. The kingdom's warriors used bronze and iron daggers and spears. Farmers had iron hoes, plowshares, and sickles. These tools helped them increase their rice crop production.

Ancient Choson had close contact with China. But China did not consider Ancient Choson an equal, independent country. In 109 B.C., the emperor of China's Han dynasty decided to expand his empire. He attacked Ancient Choson. The following year, Choson fell to the Han. China set up four territories. Each territory sent yearly tribute to China in the form of crops and other goods. In exchange for the tribute, China protected the territories from invaders. Over the course of several hundred years, this contact with China brought three important influences to Korea: the Chinese written language, Buddhism, and Confucianism. Because the Koreans had no written language, they used the Chinese writing system of ideographic characters. Buddhism eventually became the dominant religion on the peninsula. The Confucian code for organizing society and government enabled Korea's rulers to maintain order.

North Koreans and South Koreans gather to celebrate the restoration of a Buddhist temple in Kaesong, North Korea. Buddhism came to the Korean Peninsula through China.

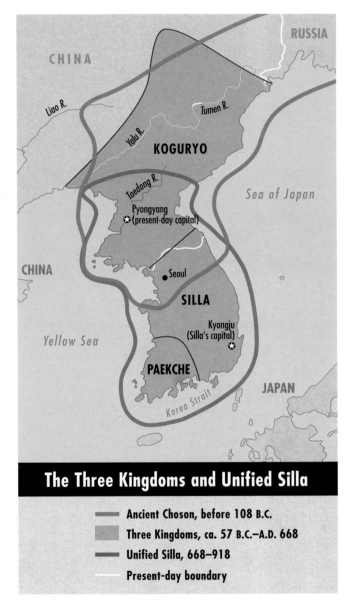

The Three Kingdoms and Unified Silla

— Ancient Choson, before 108 B.C.

▨ Three Kingdoms, ca. 57 B.C.–A.D. 668

— Unified Silla, 668–918

— Present-day boundary

The Three Kingdoms

Little by little, China lost direct control of the Korean territories. By 57 B.C., people in the northern part of the peninsula had been unified as the Koguryo Kingdom. About this time, two kingdoms were formed in southern Korea: Silla, in the southeast, and Paekche, in the southwest. Koguryo, Silla, and Paekche are known as the Three Kingdoms.

During the A.D. 300s, Koguryo adopted Buddhism and established a Confucian academy. By the 500s, the other two kingdoms had also adopted Buddhism and Confucianism. Silla also made advances in science and technology. During the mid-600s, Cheomseongdae, one of the first astronomical observatories in East Asia, was built in the Silla capital at Kyongju. The world's first woodblock printing also occurred there.

All three kingdoms sent tribute to China. They also fought with one another. Eventually, Silla formed an alliance with China's Tang dynasty. With Tang help, Silla conquered Paekche in 660 and Koguryo in 668, unifying much of the Korean Peninsula.

Unified Silla

For 250 years, Unified Silla controlled the Korean Peninsula from Pyongyang to the peninsula's southern tip. The Parhae Kingdom, which had been set up by people who had earlier pulled away from Koguryo, controlled land north of Pyongyang. Silla continued to send tribute to China, and in 735, China recognized Silla as Korea's only kingdom.

The kings of Silla set up a strict social and political order for wealthy families called the bone-rank system. A person's or family's bone rank determined their home's size; their clothing type and color; and the number of horses, carriages, and other goods they could own.

Cheomseongdae is one of the oldest structures in Korea. Its name means "Star-Gazing Tower."

Most peasant farmers owned their own land. The main crops were rice and hemp. Farmers paid taxes and had to perform free labor for the government, such as building irrigation canals and roads.

During the 700s, the Silla dynasty reached the height of its power and wealth. During this time, great Buddhist temples were built. Then, in the 800s, Silla began to break apart. Leading families began to chip away at the king's power. Peasants who were treated unfairly rebelled.

In 918, a general named Wang Kon established a new dynasty, with its capital at Kaesong. He called it Koryo. The name *Korea* comes from this dynasty's name. In 935, Wang received a formal surrender from the last Silla king. He also married a woman from the Silla royal family. Wang reunited the peninsula and extended the northern border to the mouth of the Yalu River. In 1044, a later Koryu ruler had a great wall built from the Yalu southeast to the Sea of Japan.

A monument in Kaesong honors the leaders of the Koguryo Kingdom, which ruled northern Korea from 57 B.C. to A.D. 668.

Koryo kings brought Confucian scholars into the government. Knowledge rather than rank became important as a way to advance oneself. Many cultural achievements occurred under the Koryo. Koreans developed inlaid designs in celadon pottery. They printed the entire works of Buddhist teaching using eighty-one thousand woodblocks. In 1234, they used the world's first movable metal type.

In 1231, the Mongols, a people from central Asia, invaded the Korean

Peninsula. This was the beginning of the end of the Koryo dynasty. The Mongols conquered China and established the Yuan dynasty there. Then, in 1259, they completed their conquest of Korea.

Korea's social structure fell apart under the Mongols. Korean aristocrats gained control of farmland. Peasant farmers became serfs, who no longer owned the land. They had to do the landowners' bidding. Artisans and other middle-class people became slaves. Some of these people, along with horses, ginseng, gold, and silver, were given in tribute to the Mongols. Finally, in the 1350s, the Koryo king was able to push the Mongols out of Korea.

This seated Buddha was made during the Koryo dynasty.

Korean Governments

Ancient Choson Kingdom	Prior to 108 B.C.
The Three Kingdoms	About 57 B.C.–A.D. 668
Unified Silla	668–918
Koryo dynasty	918–1392
Choson dynasty	1392–1910
Colony of Japan	1910–1945
"Temporary" division of the peninsula	1945–1948
Democratic People's Republic of Korea (North Korea)	1948–present
Republic of Korea (South Korea)	1948–present

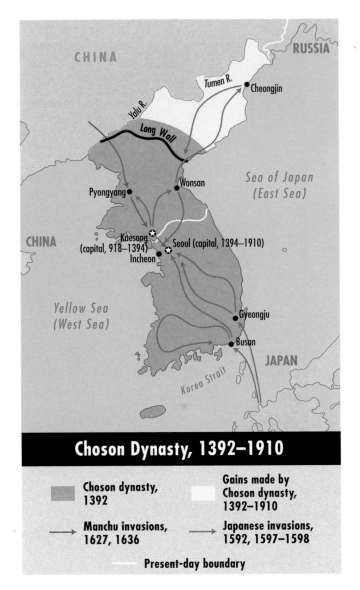

Choson Dynasty, 1392–1910

	Choson dynasty, 1392		Gains made by Choson dynasty, 1392–1910
→	Manchu invasions, 1627, 1636	→	Japanese invasions, 1592, 1597–1598
		Present-day boundary	

The map includes labels: CHINA, RUSSIA, Tumen R., Cheongjin, Yalu R., Long Wall, Wonsan, Sea of Japan (East Sea), Pyongyang, Kaesong (capital, 918–1394), Seoul (capital, 1394–1910), Incheon, Yellow Sea (West Sea), Gyeongju, Busan, JAPAN, Korea Strait.

The Choson Dynasty

With the Mongols gone and Korea in a state of decay, General Yi Song-gye seized power. In 1392, Yi was proclaimed king and established the Choson dynasty. He moved the capital from Kaesong to Seoul and began construction of a wall around the city. Yi replaced Buddhism with Confucianism as the state religion. Yi placed all Korean land under his own control. He parceled the land out to military leaders and government officials.

Yi's grandson, Sejong, reigned as king from 1418 to 1450. He is regarded as Korea's greatest ruler. Sejong extended the Korean border in the north to the Yalu and Tumen rivers, and that remains North Korea's northern border today. He encouraged inventions, such as the rain gauge. A Korean alphabet was also invented during his rule.

Sejong and later Choson kings promoted a strict Confucian social system that offered little chance for advancement. It also discouraged the development of industry and trade.

In 1592, the Japanese began a campaign to attack the Ming dynasty in China by going through Korea. They landed at Pusan and then captured Seoul and most of the peninsula. The Ming Chinese and armies of Korean landowners, peasants, and slaves united to force the Japanese out. A second unsuccessful attack began in 1597. The attacks, however, greatly weakened Korea and its government. Thousands of people died, land was destroyed, fewer crops grew, and the amount of taxes the government was able to collect decreased.

Turtle Ships

During the Japanese invasion in 1592, Korean admiral Yi Sun-sin (1545–1598) developed the world's first ironclad ships. They were called turtle ships because of their protective metal shell. Spears and arrows simply bounced off the ironclad ships. Yi had only a few ironclad ships, but they destroyed hundreds of Japanese supply ships in the Korea Strait. This helped save Korea.

In 1597, the Japanese attacked again, and once more Yi's navy defeated them. Yi was killed during one of the battles, however. Today, Yi Sun-sin is considered one of Korea's great heroes.

After recovering from the Japanese invasions, Korea was invaded from the north by the Manchus of Manchuria in 1627 and 1636. The Manchus killed many Koreans and laid waste to the land. The Choson dynasty soon surrendered and began sending tribute to the Manchus. In 1644, the Manchus overthrew the Ming dynasty in China and set up the Qing dynasty.

In response to the Japanese and Manchu invasions, the Choson dynasty closed off Korea to all countries except China. The kings built a high wooden fence across Korea's northern border. Korea became known as the Hermit Kingdom.

Christians first came to Korea in the 1600s. Here, early Korean converts to Christianity gather for services.

Between the 1640s and 1876, Korea remained isolated from the rest of the world. Korean officials sometimes met Western scholars in China. These officials brought back books about the Catholic religion. They also brought back inventions such as telescopes and alarm clocks. At the same time in Korea, a group of scholars were promoting *sirhak*, or "practical learning." These scholars were critical of parts of Confucianism's strict social code. They instead promoted social equality and the welfare of all people. They also believed that the educated should work to improve agriculture.

Korea was opened to foreign trade in the late 1800s. Here, Japanese officers (right) meet with Korean officials.

Foreigners Arrive

In 1876, Japan forced the Choson dynasty to open Korea's doors. That year, Korea opened the ports of Pusan, Inchon, and Wonsan to Japanese trade. In 1882, the United States and Korea signed a treaty establishing trade and diplomatic relations. Within the next few years, France, Germany, Great Britain, Italy, and Russia also signed treaties with Korea. Government representatives, businesspeople, and religious missionaries from those countries came to Korea. Groups from Japan and the Western countries worked to make doing business in Korea easier. They built Korea's first railroads. Telegraph and telephone lines connected Korea's main cities. Missionaries worked to make life better for the Korean people by building hospitals, schools, and universities.

By the end of the 1800s, the Choson dynasty was weak. Korea's neighbors—China, Japan, and Russia—tried to gain control of the peninsula. In 1894 and 1895, Japan fought

Japanese police officers in Korea. Hundreds of thousands of Japanese lived in Korea during the Japanese occupation.

China for influence in Korea. Japan won the war and forced China to recognize Korea as an independent country. Korea no longer had to pay tribute to China. Then, in 1904 and 1905, Japan and Russia fought for control of Korea. Again, Japan won the war. Russia recognized Japan's influence over Korea. In 1910, Japan forced King Sunjong, the last Choson king, to sign a treaty that made Korea a colony of Japan. Korea was no longer independent.

Japan Rules Korea

From 1910 to 1945, Japan ruled Korea as a colony. This meant that Korea and its people existed for the benefit of Japan. Many Japanese farmers and fishers came to work in Korea. They were given Korean farmland and rights to fish in Korean waters.

Japan began a program to strip Koreans of their national identity. Japan wanted the Koreans to become like the Japanese, although Koreans could not become Japanese citizens. The

Korean spoken and written language was replaced with Japanese. Korean language and history were no longer taught in schools. Later, the Japanese even forced the Korean people to replace their Korean names with Japanese ones. In reaction to these policies, thousands of Koreans left their homeland and migrated to China, Russia, and the Hawaiian Islands.

Some Koreans struggled against Japanese control. On March 1, 1919, Korean nationalists signed a declaration of independence that was read in the streets of Seoul, Pyongyang, and other cities. For several weeks, thousands of people throughout Korea took part in peaceful demonstrations for independence from Japan. The Japanese put down this move-

Syngman Rhee led the Korean government-in-exile during the Japanese occupation. He later served as president of South Korea for twelve years.

ment and killed about seven thousand Koreans. As a result, Korean nationalists fled to Shanghai, China, or to the newly formed communist Soviet Union, which had been known as Russia until 1917. In Shanghai, the nationalists set up the Provisional Government of the Republic of Korea. Syngman Rhee was elected president of this government-in-exile. In the 1920s, other Korean nationalists, including Kim Il Sung, turned to communism.

In the 1930s, Japan used Korea as a staging area for its invasion of Manchuria and then China. Korean crops were used to feed the Japanese army. Korean boys and men were forced to serve in the Japanese army. Other Koreans were taken to Japan to work on farms or in factories. Only in recent years has it come to light that tens of thousands of Korean women were forced to act as prostitutes for the Japanese army. Many of them died of malnutrition and disease. Those who survived lived in shame for years. North Koreans still harbor harsh feelings toward Japan because of the hardships that they endured during the time of Japanese rule.

In 1939, World War II broke out in Europe. Before this war started, Japan had formed an alliance with Germany and Italy. These countries were known as the Axis powers. Great Britain, France, and the Soviet Union, known as the Allies, opposed the Axis Powers. In 1941, the United States joined the Allies when Japan attacked Pearl Harbor in Hawai'i.

Demonstrators protest the Russian occupation of northern Korea after World War II.

United Nations forces cross the 38th Parallel in 1950. The Korean War would last three more years.

A Divided Korea and the Korean War

World War II ended in 1945 after the United States dropped atomic bombs on Japan. The Allies had previously agreed to temporarily divide the Korean Peninsula at the 38th Parallel and govern it as a trusteeship. Soviet troops marched into northern Korea and accepted the surrender of Japanese troops there. The United States accepted the surrender of Japanese troops in southern Korea.

The Soviet Union immediately closed off Korea at the 38th Parallel. They placed Korean communists in positions of power. Kim Il Sung was elected secretary of the North Korean Communist Party. He became chairman of the provisional government in the north. The U.S. military ran the government in the south. In 1948, elections supervised by the United Nations (UN) were supposed to take place in the north and in the south. The result was to be an elected national assembly for a united Korea. The Soviets, however, refused to allow UN officials into the north.

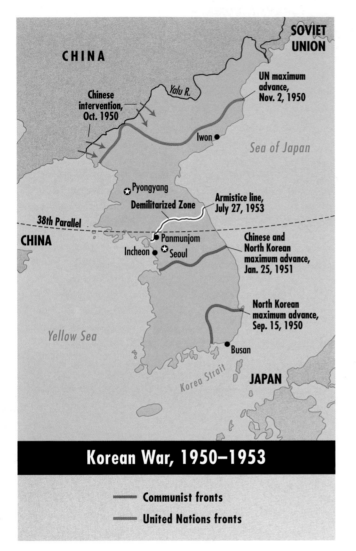

CHINA

SOVIET UNION

Chinese intervention, Oct. 1950

Yalu R.

UN maximum advance, Nov. 2, 1950

Iwon

Sea of Japan

Pyongyang

Demilitarized Zone

Armistice line, July 27, 1953

38th Parallel

CHINA

Panmunjom

Incheon • Seoul

Chinese and North Korean maximum advance, Jan. 25, 1951

North Korean maximum advance, Sep. 15, 1950

Yellow Sea

Busan

Korea Strait

JAPAN

Korean War, 1950–1953

—— Communist fronts

—— United Nations fronts

In the south, voters elected a national assembly in May 1948. The national assembly wrote a constitution and formed a government. Syngman Rhee was elected president of South Korea in July 1948, and in August the Republic of Korea was proclaimed. In the north, the Supreme People's Assembly was formed. It appointed Kim Il Sung as premier, and soon the Democratic People's Republic of Korea was proclaimed in the north. In 1949, the Soviet Union and the United States withdrew their troops from the Korean Peninsula.

Then, in June 1950, Kim Il Sung began an invasion of South Korea. His goal was to reunify Korea under his control. The United States responded by having the UN organize troops from several countries. Within a few months, UN forces had pushed the North Korean army as far as the Yalu River. Kim soon received help from the Chinese communists, who had successfully taken over China the year before. About one million communist Chinese troops joined the North Koreans and pushed the UN troops south of the 38th Parallel. A cease-fire was finally called in 1953. Though the fighting stopped, Korea remained divided at the 38th Parallel. A Demilitarized Zone (DMZ) was created across the middle of Korea. A peace treaty has never been signed officially.

At the end of the Korean War, both North Korea and South Korea lay in ruins. Farmland had been trampled, forests had been destroyed, and railroads and highways had been torn up. Many cities, including Pyongyang, had been flattened. Two million Koreans had been killed during the war. Millions more were homeless and jobless. Both countries had many years of rebuilding ahead of them.

Life Under the Kims

Kim Il Sung had imposed a communist dictatorship over North Korea. His one-man rule made progress very quickly.

At first, North Korea's economy pulled ahead of South Korea's. North Korea had most of the peninsula's mineral deposits. It also had most of the factories. The peninsula's only hydroelectric power plant was in the north. In addition, North Korea received much aid from China and the Soviet Union. Kim's government used this aid to build schools, hospitals, parks, and other facilities that improved the lives of many North Koreans.

The Korean War devastated cities and towns across the Korean Peninsula. Here, U.S. Marines file past a burning building in Kojo, North Korea.

Kim Il Sung: The "Great Leader"

Kim Il Sung ruled the Democratic People's Republic of Korea from its establishment in 1948 until his death in 1994. During his many years in power, he created a personality cult around himself. To this day, in North Korea he is officially called the "Great Leader."

Kim Il Sung was born Kim Song Ju in 1912 in the village of Mangyongdae, near Pyongyang. To escape the harsh conditions in Korea under Japanese rule, his parents fled with him to Manchuria, which was part of China. When Japan threatened to take over Manchuria, Kim joined the anti-Japanese movement. In 1930, after being jailed for taking part in protests, Kim changed his name to Kim Il Sung. Some stories say the name had belonged to a legendary Korean hero. Others say that *Il Sung* means "One Star" and was a name his comrades used for him. In 1940, after eight years of resisting the Japanese, Kim fled to the Soviet Union. He received political and military training there and served in the Soviet army during World War II. While in the Soviet Union, Kim married Kim Jong Suk. In 1942, their first son, Kim Jong Il, was born in a Soviet army camp.

When World War II ended in 1945, the Soviet Union secured the northern part of Korea and put Kim Il Sung in charge of forming the provisional government. In 1948, he became the first premier of the Democratic People's Republic of Korea.

In 1950, Kim ordered an attack on South Korea in an attempt to unite the peninsula under his control. The Korean War had begun. Although the war ended in a cease-fire with the peninsula still divided, Kim continued to grow in power. Many North Koreans remember how he made personal trips to farms, factories, and homes because he was concerned about working and living conditions. They also remember his cruelty. He established a system of concentration camps for his own people. He approved of terrorist attacks on South Korea, and he closed North Korea off from the rest of the world. When Kim Il Sung died in 1994, power passed to his son Kim Jong Il, who continues to apply his father's policies.

By 1955, Kim had established his philosophy of self-reliance, called *juche*, as the central political belief in North Korea. According to juche, North Koreans are to be politically independent and economically self-supporting. Their strong military should enable them to defend themselves without help from anyone.

Kim demanded extreme personal loyalty. Everyone was to obey him no matter what. From early childhood, Koreans were required to bow before pictures of Kim Il Sung, praising him and thanking him for taking care of them.

Kim Il Sung isolated North Korea from the rest of the world. He considered the United States to be North Korea's main enemy because of the damage done by U.S. bombs during the Korean War and because of U.S. support for the South Korean government. He also considered Japan an enemy because of the years it occupied Korea.

Throughout his life, Kim Il Sung wanted to reunite the two Koreas. In 1967 and 1968, small groups of North Koreans tried to invade South Korea, but they were stopped by South

A poster of Kim Il Sung looms over a train platform in Kaesong. Images of Kim Il Sung and Kim Jong Il are common in North Korea.

The Juche Calendar

North Korea measures the passage of years with the juche calendar. In the juche calendar, year 1 is 1912, the year of Kim Il Sung's birth. The year 2008 is juche year 97.

Millions of North Koreans went hungry in the 1990s. Here, people stand in line to receive food rations.

Korean troops. In 1968 and 1974, North Koreans attempted to assassinate South Korean president Park Chung Hee. Kim also had several tunnels dug beneath the DMZ as a way to invade South Korea. South Koreans discovered the tunnels and sealed them off. In 1983, Kim approved a terrorist attack against South Korean president Chun Doo Hwan. This assassination attempt also failed. In 1987, North Korean terrorists planted a bomb on a South Korean airline. The plane exploded in the air, killing 115 people.

In the late 1980s, North Korea's economy began to decline as its trade with other communist countries decreased. By this time, China had begun trading with the United States, South Korea, and other countries. The Soviet Union soon collapsed, and several communist governments in Eastern Europe were overthrown. Also in the late 1980s, North Koreans suffered shortages of food and fuel. These shortages resulted in years of horrifying famine during the 1990s. North Koreans call this time "the Arduous March."

Famine

In the 1990s, North Korea experienced a horrible famine. Between six hundred thousand and one million people died. What happened?

During the early 1990s, North Korea experienced a series of floods and droughts that made farming difficult. Weather alone, however, cannot explain the North Korean famine. The actions of the North Korean government also contributed to the crisis.

The government had long been making the decisions about what crops farmers would grow and where they would grow them. Local people were no longer able to decide for themselves how to keep the farmland healthy and the people fed.

Most of the forests on North Korea's hillsides had been cut down over the years to make way for fields. Without trees or plants to hold the soil in place, the soil simply washed away when heavy rains came.

North Korean farms had also long used huge amounts of some chemical fertilizers. In the short run, this increased the amount of crops grown, but in the long run, it destroyed the soil.

For many years, North Korean agriculture relied heavily on electrical irrigation systems supported by the Soviet Union. When the Soviet Union stopped giving help, the irrigation systems failed. All these elements and many more led to the famine.

Kim Il Sung died in 1994, and Kim Jong Il took over. The famine began during Kim Il Sung's lifetime, but Kim Jong Il was left to deal with it. For several years, the North Korean government denied that there was a famine. Finally, in 1995, North Korea's government called for help. The United Nations, the United States, Japan, and South Korea all sent food, but the North Korean government did not allow international groups to monitor its distribution. It is believed that much of the food did not reach the starving North Koreans.

Growing Tensions

During these economic troubles, North Korea's government continued to build its army and its arsenal of weapons, including nuclear weapons. In 1992, outside observers discovered that a nuclear power plant in North Korea could be converted to make material for nuclear weapons. South Korea stopped aid shipments to North Korea until the question of North Korea's nuclear capabilities was cleared up. In the mid-1990s, Kim Jong Il agreed to end the nuclear program and allow inspections of North Korea's nuclear power plant. In exchange, the United States and other countries agreed to build two nuclear power plants and ship much-needed fuel oil to North Korea.

In the early twenty-first century, North Korea began to open up a bit. Foreign officials such as Russian president Vladimir Putin and U.S. secretary of state Madeleine Albright met with Kim Jong Il. Some South Korean tourists were allowed to visit North Korea. North Korea and South Korea agreed to build

North Korea tested a nuclear weapon in October 2006. Many nations around the world condemned the test as provocative and dangerous.

a railway connecting the two countries. During this period, many countries, including Italy, Australia, Canada, the Netherlands, and Turkey, established diplomatic relations with North Korea.

Soon, however, North Korea's relations with other countries began to fall apart again. North Korean ships were found smuggling illegal drugs into Taiwan, Japan, and Australia. Then, in January 2003, North Korea announced that it was building nuclear weapons. A month later, North Korea test-fired a missile into the Sea of Japan. World leaders wanted to get North Korea to stop its nuclear program. South Korea, Russia, Japan, China, and the United States began talks with North Korea.

In 2003, North Korea took part in talks with representatives of nearby nations and the United States to try to ease tensions.

North Korea pulled out of the six-party talks in late 2005. Tensions increased further as North Korea test-fired several more missiles over the Sea of Japan and then conducted an underground nuclear weapons test. More talks were held. Agreements were made and broken. In 2007, North Korea agreed to end its nuclear program in exchange for U.S. aid. That same year, leaders of North Korea and South Korea held a summit. Still, North Korea remains an unpredictable and dangerous actor on the world stage.

CHAPTER

FIVE

Dictatorship

58

NORTH KOREA'S CONSTITUTION GUARANTEES FREEDOM of speech, the press, and religion. It also calls for the election of government leaders. The people in North Korea have no real freedom, however, and virtually all candidates come from North Korea's one major political party—the Korean Workers' Party (KWP). In other words, North Korea is a dictatorship.

At first, Kim Il Sung's dictatorship was based on the same ideas as the communist dictatorships in the Soviet Union and China. Later, his dictatorship became more nationalistic. Under nationalism, the government tells the people that their nation is the best and that they themselves are superior

Opposite: **A portrait of Kim Il Sung is held high during a huge military parade in Pyongyang. North Korea has the fourth-largest military in the world.**

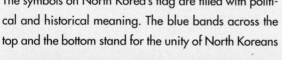

North Korea's Flag

The symbols on North Korea's flag are filled with political and historical meaning. The blue bands across the top and the bottom stand for the unity of North Koreans

with people around the world in the fight for independence, peace, and friendship. The two narrow white bands represent Korea's ancient culture and heroic people. The red band represents the patriotism of people who died fighting to reunite Korea during the Korean War. The white circle symbolizes the North Korean people, while the red star stands for the revolutionary ideas of Kim Il Sung.

to everyone else. North Koreans are taught to believe this. Because the government considers North Koreans superior, it does not allow marriages between North Koreans and people from other countries.

The National Government

In North Korea, government power is supposed to rest with the one-house legislature called the Supreme People's Assembly (SPA). Its 687 members are elected for five-year terms from a single list of candidates. The SPA meets only a few days each year. At that time, it approves decisions already made by the KWP. All of North Korea's leaders must belong to this political party.

The president of the SPA is supposedly the head of the government, but the real control of North Korea's government lies with leaders of the KWP and the military. The chairman of the National Defense Commission, Kim Jong Il, is the head of both of those groups. The chairman rules the country with the help of the State Administrative Council.

NATIONAL GOVERNMENT OF NORTH KOREA

Executive Branch

CHAIRMAN OF THE NATIONAL DEFENSE COMMISSION

STATE ADMINISTRATIVE COUNCIL

Legislative Branch

SUPREME PEOPLE'S ASSEMBLY

Judicial Branch

CENTRAL COURT

North Korea's judicial system consists of the Central Court, provincial courts, and people's courts at the city and county levels. All judges and justices are also members of the KWP.

Kim Jong Il: The "Dear Leader"

Kim Jong Il holds complete power in North Korea. He is chairman of the National Defense Commission, general secretary of the Korean Workers' Party, and supreme commander of the People's Army.

Kim Jong Il was born on February 16, 1942, in an army camp in the Soviet Union, where his parents, Kim Il Sung and Kim Jong Suk, were part of the Soviet army during World War II. North Korean stories, however, say that he was born in a log cabin on Mount Paektu—the birthplace of Tangun, the legendary founder of the Ancient Choson Kingdom. Thus, say the stories, Kim Jong Il was fated to be the leader of the North Korean people.

After Kim Jong Il grew up, he began working closely with his father. He is believed to have played a leading role in a failed 1983 assassination attempt on South Korea's president. He is also believed to have helped plan the 1987 midair explosion of a South Korean jet that killed 115 people.

Many years before Kim Il Sung died, he began preparing his son to succeed him in power. This was in keeping with previous Korean dynasties, but it was the first time in a communist country that a son had followed his father as the country's leader.

Kim Jong Il officially took power in 1997, three years after the death of his father. Kim surrounds himself with loyal supporters who dare not contradict him. He makes few speeches and travels little outside of North Korea. Kim is known for his extravagant lifestyle. He moves among many mansions in the North Korean mountains and along the seacoast. He has a fleet of Mercedes cars and a collection of twenty thousand movies.

Kim will do whatever is necessary to remain in power. During his regime, he has built up the military and increased a system of spying aimed at the North Korean people.

In North Korea, Kim Jong Il is officially called "Dear Leader," but he is a ruthless ruler. He will likely be remembered for ruling North Korea during the great famine of the 1990s and for taunting South Korea, the United States, and other countries with threats of making nuclear weapons.

From Palace to Tomb

North Korea's presidential palace has been renamed the Kumsusan Memorial Palace. Kim Il Sung was the only president to live in the palace. Now, it is his final resting place. Kim's embalmed body is on display there.

Local Government

North Korea has nine provinces that are divided into cities and counties. The city of Pyongyang functions like a province.

People's assemblies and people's committees are elected at all levels of local government. These assemblies and committees have no real power, however. They carry out KWP regulations related to all political, economic, and cultural activities. This includes hiring spies to keep an eye on other people. The spies make sure that people are doing their work, that they are not getting more rations than they should, and that they are not listening to or viewing illegal broadcasts.

Students sing and dance in front of portraits of Kim Il Sung and Kim Jong Il. Pictures of the leaders hang in all North Korean classrooms.

The National Anthem

North Korea's national anthem was adopted in 1947, a year before the country was established.

Let morning shine on the silver and gold of this land,
Three thousand leagues packed with natural wealth.
My beautiful fatherland.
The glory of a wise people
Brought up in a culture brilliant
With a history five millennia long.
Let us devote our bodies and minds
To supporting this Korea forever.

The firm will, bonded with truth,
Nest for the spirit of labor,
Embracing the atmosphere of Mount Paektu,
Will go forth to all the world.
The country established by the will of the people,
Breasting the raging waves with soaring strength.
Let us glorify forever this Korea,
Limitlessly rich and strong.

The People's Rights

All North Korean citizens at least seventeen years old have the right to vote. Although the constitution grants them many other rights, North Koreans really have no rights at all. The press is censored. Free speech is not allowed. There is no freedom of religion, although some temples remain open as show for tourists. North Koreans cannot leave the country or freely move about within it.

Worst of all is the plight of the more than two hundred thousand political prisoners held in isolated camps in the northern mountains. There, prisoners work twelve hours a day, seven days a week. They are held until they die or until they convince prison officials that they have become faithful followers of Kim Jong Il and the idea of juche.

Military Forces

North Korea has the world's fourth-largest military force, with about 1.2 million soldiers, sailors, and airmen. All males between the ages of seventeen and twenty-eight are required to serve in the military for three to eight years. According to some estimates, North Korea spends at least 28 percent of its gross domestic product—the total value of all goods and services produced in the country—on military costs. The United States, in contrast, spends about 3.7 percent.

Another 4.7 million North Koreans are in the military reserves. Because they can be called to serve at any time, they drill frequently, practicing with sticks instead of guns. Even schoolchildren march and drill. Supposedly, all North Korean people are prepared to fight and die for their "Dear Leader."

Kim Jong Il (center) is both North Korea's political leader and the supreme commander of the Korean People's Army.

Pyongyang: Did You Know This?

Pyongyang is located on the Taedong River in south-western North Korea. About 36 inches (92 cm) of rain falls on Pyongyang each year. Average temperatures range from 18 degrees Fahrenheit (-8 degrees Celcius) in January to 75°F (24°C) in July.

According to legend, Pyongyang was founded in 2333 B.C. by Tangun. In A.D. 427, Pyongyang became the capital of the Koguryo Kingdom. Today, it is North Korea's largest city, with a population of about 3,136,000. Pyongyang is the political, economic,

cultural, and educational center of the country. Main industries include the production of chemicals, iron and steel, sugar, textiles, and electrical equipment. Major attractions include huge monuments to Kim Il Sung, two old city gates, the Tower of the Juche Idea, Kim Il Sung Square, and the Korean Revolution Museum (above).

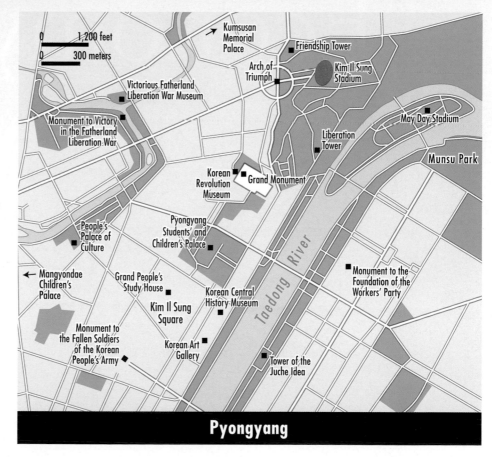

0   1,200 feet
0   300 meters

Kumsusan Memorial Palace

Friendship Tower

Arch of Triumph

Kim Il Sung Stadium

Victorious Fatherland Liberation War Museum

May Day Stadium

Monument to Victory in the Fatherland Liberation War

Liberation Tower

Munsu Park

Korean Revolution Museum

Grand Monument

People's Palace of Culture

Pyongyang Students' and Children's Palace

Taedong River

Monument to the Foundation of the Workers' Party

← Mangyondae Children's Palace

Grand People's Study House

Korean Central History Museum

Kim Il Sung Square

Monument to the Fallen Soldiers of the Korean People's Army

Korean Art Gallery

Tower of the Juche Idea

Pyongyang

A Controlled Economy

NORTH KOREA'S ECONOMY IS CONTROLLED BY THE GOVERNMENT. The government owns all the land, factories, and housing. It determines what and how much is grown, produced, exported, and imported. The government determines how food is rationed and who lives in what kind of housing.

Since the 1990s, North Korea's economy has been in crisis. In the mid-1990s, floods and droughts ruined North Korea's crops. This led to a famine throughout the country. Desperate

Opposite: **Workers in Nampo unload sacks of wheat.**

Women harvesting rice. North Korea does not grow enough rice to feed its people, so it imports a great deal.

people were forced to eat grass, seeds, and tree bark. Because the government was slow to react and didn't ask for help from other countries, it is estimated that between six hundred thousand and one million people died from starvation. A decade later, North Korea was still recovering from the famine.

The North Korean government lacks the funds needed to import fuel oil. As a result, most farming is done by hand and with draft animals rather than with machinery. Because of the fuel shortage, some factories have had to shut down or cut back on hours. In addition, low fuel levels leave most North Koreans living in cold, dark homes.

Farming and Fishing

About 30 percent of North Koreans work as farmers on state-owned farms. Rice is the main crop, but North Korea

North Korea's Currency

The currency in North Korea is called the won. Paper money comes in values of 1, 5, 10, 50, 100, 200, 500, 1,000, and 5,000 won. Coins come in values of 1, 5, 10, and 50 won. North Korea's colorful money displays images of workers and people or places of historical or cultural importance. For example, the 5,000-won note shows Kim Il Sung on the front and his birthplace on the back. The 200-won note has an image of the national flower. In 2007, US$1 equaled 142 won.

North Korea's political and military leaders have access to U.S. dollars, which they use to buy luxury goods in stores set up for diplomats from other countries.

A farmer shows how high corn normally grows. Drought had stunted that year's crop.

produces less than half the amount of rice needed to feed its people. Rice does not grow well in North Korea. Potatoes, corn, barley, and wheat grow better there. In recent years, the government has encouraged farmers to plant and harvest more of those crops. In some areas, farmers also grow fruits, such as apples, peaches, pears, and melons. Much of the fruit crop is exported, however. Farmers also raise a small number of cattle, hogs, and chickens. In 2005, an outbreak of bird flu hit farms near Pyongyang and Kaesong. About 218,000 chickens had to be destroyed to prevent the bird flu from spreading.

Fishing makes up a small but important part of North Korea's economy. Along the Sea of Japan, abalones, cod, king crabs, pollack, and squid are plentiful. The waters of the Yellow Sea provide blue crabs, lobsters, shrimps, and surf

What North Korea Grows, Makes, and Mines

Agriculture (2004)

Rice	2,370,000 metric tons
Potatoes	2,052,000 metric tons
Corn	1,727,000 metric tons

Manufacturing

Cement (2002)	53,200,000 metric tons
Crude steel (2002)	10,400,000 metric tons
Pig iron (1999)	6,600,000 metric tons

Mining

Coal (2002)	50,700,000 metric tons
Iron ore (2003)	1,260,000 metric tons
Magnesite (2003)	1,000,000 metric tons

clams. Much of the catch is exported. The government has recently encouraged the cultivation of mudfish, which are also called loach. The mudfish are easy to raise and are rich in vitamins and protein. An increase in mudfish production may help improve nutrition among North Koreans.

Mining and Energy

North Korea is fortunate to have most of the Korean Peninsula's mineral resources. High-grade iron ore deposits are mined near the southwest coast. Rich deposits of anthracite coal lie along the northern reaches of the Taedong River. Lignite coal is found in the Tumen River basin. North Korea also mines magnesite, phosphate rock, tungsten, sulfur, zinc, lead, gold, silver, and copper.

About 80 percent of North Korea's electric power comes from burning coal. Hydroelectric power plants supply about 12 percent of the nation's power. North Korea's one nuclear power plant, along with oil and natural gas, provide the rest of the country's electric power.

Manufacturing

About 30 percent of North Korean workers make goods in factories. The main products are cement and steel. These products are used to construct plazas for national monuments, buildings, and roads. North Korea also produces a great deal of chemicals and heavy machinery, including bulldozers, locomotives, engines, generators, and military equipment and weapons. Consumer goods such as food products, clothing, and shoes account for a small part of North Korea's economy.

In 2003, Hyundai, a large South Korean corporation, established an industrial park near Kaesong, North Korea. About nine hundred South Korean manufacturing companies plan to build factories in the park. By 2007, about forty South Korean factories had opened in the industrial park. They

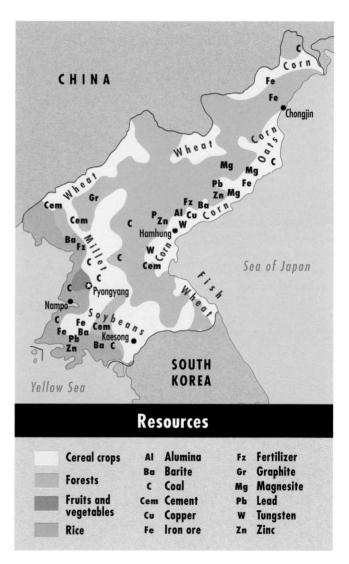

Resources

Cereal crops	Al Alumina	Fz Fertilizer
Forests	Ba Barite	Gr Graphite
	C Coal	Mg Magnesite
Fruits and vegetables	Cem Cement	Pb Lead
	Cu Copper	W Tungsten
Rice	Fe Iron ore	Zn Zinc

employed about 15,000 North Koreans making goods such as clothes and shoes. Eventually, the industrial park is supposed to provide 730,000 North Koreans with jobs. The workers are paid an amount equal to about US$70 a month. Most of the money goes to the North Korean government, however. After the government takes out deductions, the workers are believed to receive about US$10 a month. This is still more than a worker in a regular North Korean factory receives.

Trade and Tourism

Trade is important to the North Korean economy. The country's major exports include lead, magnesite, zinc, cement, and fish. Its main imports are coal, machinery for factories and

Workers make bicycles at a factory in Pyongyang. Bicycles are the major means of transportation in North Korea.

transportation, textiles, and food grains. North Korea's main trading partners are China, Japan, and South Korea. The value of North Korea's exports is much less than the value of its imports.

Tourism is slowly becoming important to North Korea. In 1998, the first South Korean tourists arrived in North Korea on a tour organized by the Hyundai Corporation. Their destination was the Kumgang Mountain tourist resort. Tourists from other countries enter North Korea from China. Individual tourists are limited to sightseeing in the city of Pyongyang. Groups of tourists, however, are allowed to visit the Kumgang Mountains, Mount Myohyang National Park, Mount Paektu, and the beaches at Nampo.

Kumgang Mountain is one of the first places in North Korea opened to foreign tourists.

Growing Markets

Since the 1990s, private markets have been opening in cities and towns. During the famine, the government could not provide food, clothing, and other goods, so some people—mainly women—began to provide these goods themselves. At first, items were traded for other goods. Now goods are sold for North Korean won. Some enterprising North Koreans have set up stalls near popular tourist sites. They are paid in Chinese yuan or European euros.

System of Weights and Measures

North Korea officially uses the metric system of weights and measures. Traditional weights and measures are also used. For example, North Koreans measure length in a unit called *ri*. One ri is the same as 12,884 feet or 3,927 meters.

A South Korean soldier watches as a North Korean train crosses the DMZ into South Korea.

Railroads and highways connect major cities and towns around North Korea. Although the country has approximately 19,400 miles (31,200 km) of highways, only about 6 percent of the roads are paved. Most of the 262,000 cars in North Korea are owned by high-ranking officials. In recent years, ordinary citizens with enough money have been able to buy used cars. Because North Korea has so few cars, traffic is never a problem. Two highways now cut across the DMZ. One ends at the industrial park in Kaesong. The other crosses the eastern DMZ, carrying South Korean tourists into North Korea.

In 2000, work began to rebuild two stretches of railroad track that would link North Korea to South Korea. In May 2007, the first trains ran on these tracks. In the east, a train from North Korea traveled across the DMZ to Chejin in South Korea. In the west, a train left Munsan, South Korea, headed for Kaesong, North Korea.

Communications

In North Korea, the government censors all information that appears in newspapers and on the radio and television. Through the media, the government instills its philosophy of juche and spreads its version of events. During the famine, the government used the media to blame the food shortage on the weather and on U.S. policies.

Many North Korean homes now have telephones, but they are not connected to all the other phones in the country. In addition, ordinary citizens cannot call outside North Korea. Internet connections are also limited. Only high-ranking officials have Web access. Cell phones are forbidden in North Korea, even among visitors. Tourists must turn over their cell phones, pagers, and other communication devices when they enter the country. The devices are returned to the visitors when they leave North Korea.

North Korea has a small but flourishing computer industry. More and more computer software is being developed there.

Being Korean

North Koreans on a bus wave good-bye after a visit with their South Korean relatives.

Τ HE NORTH KOREAN PEOPLE CAN TRACE THEIR ANCESTRY back to the central Asian people who migrated to the Korean Peninsula about five thousand years ago. Today's North Koreans are an ethnically homogeneous group. That means that they have mixed little with people of other backgrounds. People who are not ethnically Korean account for less than 1 percent of the people in North Korea. A few people from China and Japan live permanently in North Korea. A very few from other countries also live in North Korea, but on a temporary basis. Most are representing their governments or work for foreign companies.

Opposite: **Posters promoting North Korean power and self-reliance cover a wall in Pyongyang.**

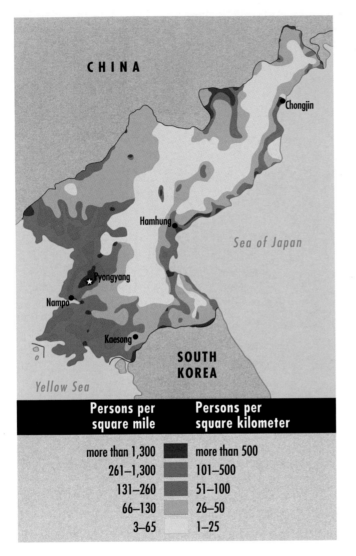

Persons per square mile		Persons per square kilometer
more than 1,300		more than 500
261–1,300		101–500
131–260		51–100
66–130		26–50
3–65		1–25

In 2007, North Korea's population was estimated to be 23,301,725. More than 60 percent of North Koreans live in urban areas. Most of the rest of the population live in farming villages along the coastal plains. Only about a quarter of the people live in the mountains, even though mountains cover 80 percent of the land.

Leaving Korea

In the early twentieth century, many Koreans immigrated to the United States. The first Korean immigrants arrived on the U.S.-controlled Hawaiian Islands and worked on sugar and pineapple plantations. After the Korean War, many more Koreans left their war-torn land to make homes on the mainland of the United States. Today, a few million Koreans and people of Korean descent live in U.S. cities such as Los Angeles, New York, Chicago, and Seattle. Many have roots in what is now North Korea. Several thousand Koreans also live in Japan. Their families had been moved there while Japan occupied the peninsula.

North Korea does not allow its people to move out of the country. The only way out is by escaping over the Chinese or Russian border, through the mine-laden DMZ, or by boat to Japan. In 2006, an estimated forty thousand to fifty thousand North Koreans were believed to be hiding in China. If they are found, the Chinese government returns them to North Korea. Some commit suicide rather than go home. Several thousand North Koreans also live in the border areas of Russia. Some are recent escapees, while others have lived there since the 1930s.

In 2006, a record two thousand North Koreans reached freedom and safety in South Korea. In June 2007, four members of a fishing family traveled about 550 miles (900 km) in a small fishing boat from North Korea to Japan. They were on the water for six days. The South Korean government has agreed to take them in.

Population of Major North Korean Cities

Pyongyang (1999 est.)	3,136,000
Nampo (1993 est.)	731,448
Hamhung (1993 est.)	709,730
Chongjin (1993 est.)	582,480
Kaesong (1993 est.)	334,433

Korean signs hang from buildings in New York City's Koreatown. New York has the second-largest Korean American population in the United States, trailing only Los Angeles.

The North Korean government also refuses to allow outsiders to move into North Korea. In the past thirty years, a small number of people have fled from South Korea into North Korea. A few were U.S. soldiers who had committed crimes in South Korea and thought they would have an easier time in North Korea.

The Korean Language

All North Koreans speak the same language. Spoken Korean is not clearly related to either Chinese or Japanese, although it has adopted many words from these languages. It belongs to a language group of central Asia. Japanese, Turkish, and

Creating an Alphabet

During the 1400s, King Sejong had his scholars create an alphabet for the Korean language. Until that time, Koreans used Chinese characters when writing. The Chinese written language has thousands of characters. Instead of putting together a few letters to form many words, the Chinese have a separate character for each word or idea. This made learning written Chinese difficult. In Sejong's time, only scholars could read and write. Sejong wanted more of his people to have the pleasure of reading and writing.

Sejong's scholars developed the *hanguel* alphabet, called *choson muncha* in North Korea. At first, only women and common people used this alphabet. Scholars continued to use Chinese characters. After World War II, choson muncha became the official written language of North Korea.

classic Mongolian also belong to this group. Although there is only one Korean language, there are several North Korean dialects, or spoken versions, of Korean. Most North Koreans can easily understand all the dialects.

Written Korean looks quite different from English. Most European languages, such as English, are written using the letters of the Latin alphabet. The Korean language, however, uses the *hangeul* alphabet, which is called *choson muncha* in North Korea. This alphabet has ten vowels and fourteen consonants. There are no letters or sounds for the *f, q, v, w, x,* and *z* of the Latin alphabet. In North Korea, choson muncha uses accent marks and apostrophes to indicate the pronunciation of some vowels. (In this book, the North Korean spellings are used without the accents and apostrophes.)

The Choson Muncha Alphabet

Choson Muncha Vowels	English Vowels	Choson Muncha Consonants	English Consonants
ㅏ	a	ㄱ	g, k
ㅑ	ya	ㄴ	n
ㅓ	eo	ㄷ	d, t
ㅕ	yeo	ㄹ	r, l
ㅗ	o	ㅁ	m
ㅛ	yo	ㅂ	b/p
ㅜ	u	ㅅ	s
ㅠ	yu	ㅇ	ng
ㅡ	eu	ㅈ	j
ㅣ	i	ㅊ	ch
		ㅋ	k
		ㅌ	t
		ㅍ	p
		ㅎ	h

A sign written using the choson muncha alphabet

In South Korea, many Chinese characters are also used in writing. North Koreans use only the choson muncha alphabet. Doing away with Chinese characters and Chinese words is part of the juche philosophy of self-reliance.

Korean Names

Korean names usually have three parts. The family name comes first. The second part is a generation name, which is shared by all family members of the same sex in the same generation. The third part is a given, or personal, name. In North Korea, each of the three names is capitalized, as in the name Kim Jong Il.

A married woman does not take her husband's family name. If a woman is called Mrs. Kim, that means she's married and that her father's family name is Kim.

Women are usually called by their relationship to their husband or children. For example, if Mrs. Kim was married to Mr. Park, she would be known as Mr. Park's wife. When Mrs. Kim becomes a mother, she will be known by the name of her oldest child.

Koreans rarely use given names when talking to each other. They usually use titles, such as Mrs., Mr., Director, Supervisor, or Principal, or they refer to each other by their station in the family, such as Elder Sister or Younger Brother.

Education and Health

Education is important in North Korea. Virtually everyone in the country can read and write. North Korean children must attend school for eleven years, starting at age five. They study math, the Korean language, English, history, and science. They take part in physical education, and boys are trained in marching. North Korean schools also teach children about the life and ideas of Kim Il Sung and Kim Jong Il and about the juche philosophy. Each day starts with the students swearing an oath of loyalty to the Kims and to the country. Pictures of the two Kims hang in every classroom.

Children in North Korea wear uniforms to school.

Kim Il Sung University, which was founded in 1946 in Pyongyang, is the country's most prestigious university. Difficult entrance examinations determine who will attend the school. The nation also has many other universities and technical and agricultural colleges. The North Korean government pays for all levels of education.

The government also pays for all health care. In recent years, North Korea has suffered severe shortages of medicine and medical equipment. In some hospitals, however, state-of-the-art equipment stands untouched because the doctors and nurses do not know how to use it.

A North Korean doctor measures out medicine. North Korea's health care system is not well funded, and only the country's elite receive good care.

Since the famine of the 1990s, North Korea has had a higher infant mortality rate and a lower average life expectancy. Food shortages have stunted the growth of many North Korean children. For example, an average seven-year-old in South Korea is about 49 inches (125 centimeters) tall and weighs about 57 pounds (26 kilograms). But the average seven-year-old in North Korea is just 45 inches (115 cm) tall and weighs only 35 pounds (16 kg). Doctors continue to worry about the long-term effects of malnutrition in North Korea.

Many children in North Korea are small because they do not get enough to eat. An estimated 37 percent of children under age six are malnourished.

A Rein on Religion

Although North Korea's constitution guarantees freedom of religion, the government controls religion. For the most part, religious worship is not allowed in North Korea, and religious holidays are not celebrated. Some religious practices that are not approved by the government are conducted in secret. In some ways, the veneration of Kim Il Sung and Kim Jong Il has become the unofficial state religion of North Korea.

Opposite: **A Buddhist pagoda towers over the countryside in Kaesong.**

A woman puts flowers in front of a picture of Kim Jong Il (left) and his father, Kim Il Sung.

Religions in North Korea

Cheondogyo	14%
Traditional religions	14%
Buddhism	2%
Christianity	1%
Other or no religion	69%

Although religious practice is tightly controlled in North Korea, Korea has a rich religious heritage incorporating many belief systems. These include Shamanism, Buddhism, Confucianism, Daoism, Christianity, and Cheondogyo. Many of these religions began elsewhere. Buddhism began in India and came to Korea through China. Confucianism and Daoism came directly from China. Christianity first came to Korea through China. Then, missionaries from Europe and the United States set up churches on the Korean Peninsula. Cheondogyo was created in Korea in reaction to Western learning and religions.

A Christian hymnbook written in Korean. Only a handful of churches are allowed to operate in Pyongyang.

Shamanists believe that trees, mountains, and other parts of nature have spirits.

Ancient Belief Systems

Shamanism is North Korea's oldest religion. It has been practiced since ancient times. The center of Shamanism is the shaman, or *mudang*. Today, as in the past, the mudang is usually a woman who acts as a link, a negotiator, between the living and the dead. Through a ceremony called *kut*, the mudang contacts spirits. During the ceremony, the mudang goes into a trance. It is believed that while in this trance, the mudang can see the future, cast out evil spirits, and ask for good fortune from the kind spirits.

Shamanism holds that all things have spirits or souls. This includes rocks, trees, streams, and mountains. Small shaman shrines were once found beneath trees and beside streams in North Korea. Shaman spirit posts carved with scary faces—they look something like totem poles—once stood at the entrance to small villages. They were supposed to keep evil out of the villages. Today, few people practice Shamanism in North Korea. Most mudangs fled to South Korea after the Korean War.

Daoism is based on the ideas of the philosopher Laozi. His name means "Old Master."

Daoism is another belief that is based on nature. *Dao*, which means "the Way," is more a philosophy than a religion. The philosopher Laozi began this belief system in China in the 500s B.C. Daoism had reached Korea by the 100s B.C. Through Daoism, people are supposed to gain an understanding of nature's laws and come to live in harmony with nature. This leads to prosperity and long life. Few North Koreans practice Daoism today.

Confucianism

Confucianism is not a religion like Buddhism or Christianity. There are no priests or monks, no god, no churches, and no worship rituals. Instead, Confucianism is a system of relationships with a code of behavior. When followed, this system ensures a well-ordered society. Confucius (551–479 B.C.), a Chinese teacher and philosopher, developed this code of conduct. According to Confucius, there are five ranks of relationships: ruler/subject or government/citizen, father/son, older person/younger person, husband/wife, and friend/friend. In each relationship, the weaker or younger person submits to the stronger or older person. The stronger person is obliged to protect the weaker one. According to Confucianism, equality exists only in the relationship between friends, and then only if the two people are the same age and gender.

In Confucianism, respect for one's elders leads to respect for ancestors. Thus, Confucianism also calls for special ceremonies of ancestor worship. At one time, Confucianism required that government officials be scholars who had passed a rigorous civil service examination. To prepare for this test, young men spent years studying in Confucian academies.

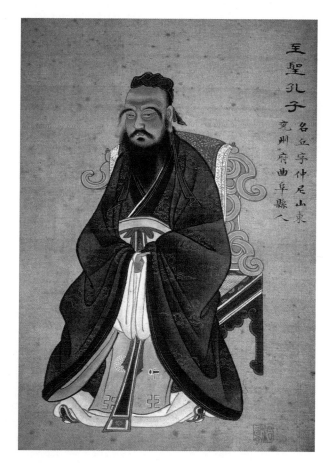

Confucius was born in Shandong Province, a coastal region of China. His teachings stressed personal morality and the proper behavior of governments.

A Rein on Religion **93**

Historians believe that Confucianism was introduced to Korea in the first centuries A.D. Later, it became the official philosophy or state religion of the Choson dynasty. Koreans followed Confucianism so strictly that Chinese visitors said that Korea was more Confucian than China. Today, North Koreans still practice the ideas of Confucius. They have to show respect to their parents, honor their ancestors, maintain strong ties with all their relatives, and show loyalty to their work unit or school. The leaders of North Korea have used Confucian traditions to keep the people loyal to them and to their government. Through Confucianism, North Koreans have a strong sense of community. When something bad happens, such as the famine of the 1990s, everyone in the country works together.

During the floods and famine of the 1990s, many North Koreans worked together to help stop hills from eroding.

Buddhism

Buddhism was founded in India in about 528 B.C. by Siddhartha Gautama. He was later called the Buddha, "the Enlightened One." Enlightenment is the goal of all Buddhists. Enlightenment is achieved when a person eliminates all desire. Buddhists believe desire is the cause of all suffering. Until people attain enlightenment, they must go through a cycle of birth, death, and rebirth known as reincarnation. Besides the Buddha, there are many gods and goddesses in the Buddhist religion.

Buddhism entered Korea from China in the A.D. 300s. It became the state religion in each of the Three Kingdoms, as well as in Unified Silla, and the Koryo dynasty. Although several Buddhist temples remain in North Korea, they are now under government control and are used for nonreligious purposes. In recent years, the government has allowed the establishment of a Buddhist academy and services in a few temples.

Many Buddhist temples built during the Choson dynasty include carved figures of boy attendants.

The Holy Valley Temple

In 2004, Buddhist monks from South Korea started to rebuild a temple on Mount Kumgang in North Korea. With money from the South Korean government, they are reconstructing fourteen buildings in the temple complex. The North Korean government approved this rebuilding because it is in a popular tourist area. Kim Il Sung is said to have visited the temple in 1947 and praised its rooflines.

Christianity also first reached Korea through China. This religion teaches that Jesus Christ is the son of God and that he died to redeem the sins of all people. During the 1600s, officials of the Choson dynasty carried Catholic writings into Korea. In 1784, the first Roman Catholic priests arrived in Korea. The government did not approve of Catholicism because Catholics were not allowed to take part in ancestor worship. In the early 1800s, thousands of Korean Catholics were executed.

Jongbaek Church is the only Russian Orthodox church in North Korea. It was established in 2006.

In the late 1800s, after Korea had opened to trade with other countries, Protestant missionaries from England and the United States arrived. Both Catholic and Protestant missionaries established schools, universities, hospitals, and orphanages. Many missionary groups had their headquarters in Pyongyang.

During the Japanese occupation, Christian missionaries worked with Koreans to win back Korea's independence. At that time, Pyongyang had a large Christian population and was thought of as one of Asia's major Christian cities.

After North Korea was established, Christians fled to the south to avoid persecution and execution. Today, a small number of Christians remain in North Korea. In the 1980s, a large Roman Catholic church and two Protestant churches were built in Pyongyang. In the late 1980s, Kim Il Sung invited American minister Billy Graham to preach in one of the Protestant churches. Many observers believe that only selected people are allowed to worship in these churches. They argue that they are just there to give the impression that North Korea allows religious freedom.

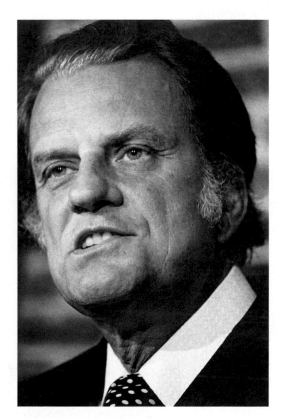

Billy Graham preached in North Korea twice at the invitation of Kim Il Sung. His wife, Ruth Graham, went to high school in Pyongyang in the 1930s, when her parents were missionaries.

Cheondogyo

In the 1860s, Choe Je-u began the Donghak Movement, or Eastern Learning Movement. This was in reaction to the Western learning that was being spread through Korea by

Buddhism greatly influenced Cheondogyo. This ancient Korean Buddhist statue was made during the Koryo dynasty.

the Catholic Church. The government executed Choe in 1863, but his movement continued to gain followers. They changed the movement's name to Cheondogyo, "Teachings of the Heavenly Way." The main beliefs of Cheondogyo are that all people are equal and that there is divinity or God in each person.

Today, Cheondogyo is the largest religion in North Korea, with about three million believers. The government has allowed it to grow because it began in Korea as a movement among poor farmers.

Traditional and Modern Culture

NORTH KOREANS TREASURE THEIR RICH CULTURAL traditions in the arts and in sports. North Korean leaders have promoted the idea that Korea and Koreans are superior to other countries and other people. As proof of this superiority, North Koreans point to traditional Korean arts, crafts, and sports.

Opposite: **North Korean children learn gymnastics and other skills in classes after school.**

Girls learn the art of embroidery at the Mangyongdae Children's Palace.

Training in the traditional arts and sports begins with young children. The Mangyongdae Children's Palace in Pyongyang is a center for after-school activities. Children learn the moves of *taekwondo* and other traditional sports. They are also taught to play traditional Korean musical instruments and are trained in the techniques of painting and drawing. Talented children in all parts of the country are given artistic training in their own towns or cities.

Girls learn traditional dances at the Mangyongdae Children's Palace in Pyongyang.

Performers wear masks during some traditional Korean dances. This mask dates back to the 1600s.

Performing Arts

North Koreans enjoy traditional, classical, and popular music. From a young age, children are molded into singers. They sometimes perform in large groups. They perfect their sound and accompanying movements so that several hundred singers can perform as one mind, one body, one voice. In rural areas, these groups perform for farmers and groups of workers. Some North Korean singers also perform solo or in small groups. Solo singing competitions are popular on North Korean television.

Young girls learning to play the gayageum. This instrument dates back about 1,500 years.

North Koreans are also trained to play traditional instruments. Groups of singers often use the *gayageum*, a twelve-string zither, as accompaniment. Other stringed instruments include the *ajaeng*, a seven-string zither, and the *haegeum*, a two-string fiddle. Korean percussion instruments include the *buk* (barrel drum), the *kkwaenggwari* (small gong), the *jing* (large gong), and the *janggo* (hourglass drum). Drums and gongs are played by dancers during folk dances, as well as by drum and gong ensembles. Korean wind instruments are played in groups with other instruments. The main wind instruments are the *daegeum* (large bamboo flute), the *hojeok* (conical oboe), the *piri* (bamboo oboe), and the *tungso* (bamboo vertical flute).

Many North Korean children also learn to play nontraditional instruments, such as the accordion and the guitar. They play at special performances and entertain their families at home. Most modern songs are based on political ideals, and many praise Kim Il Sung and Kim Jong Il. The children of high-ranking officials have some access to popular music from South Korea, China, and the United States.

Traditional dances include folk, court, and religious performances. *Pulgmulnori* is a popular farmers' dance. The dancers' hats have long streamers, which the dancers swirl in wide

North Korean dancers perform at an event celebrating the anniversary of the communist party in North Korea.

loops. During some folk dances, performers wear large, full-head masks with exaggerated expressions. In the past, the dancers wore masks to hide their identity because they were making fun of the ruling class. Today, the dances are performed as entertainment. *Taepyeongmu* ("Dance of Great Peace") is a court dance from the Choson dynasty. It is performed in the name of national peace and prosperity.

North Koreans perform a traditional dance at a ceremony marking the end of Japanese colonial rule.

The Koguryo Tombs

The Koguryo Tombs Complex in western North Korea is among the most important cultural sites in the entire country. The complex includes about thirty graves dating from the 200s B.C. to the A.D. 600s. The tombs belonged to kings or other members of the royal family. Many of the tombs are decorated with beautiful wall paintings. The paintings offer a rare view into everyday life in the Koguryo Kingdom.

Filmmaking

Koreans have been making films since 1919, with the production of a drama called *Righteous Revenge*. Under Kim Il Sung, the Pyongyang Film Studios were built on the outskirts of Pyongyang. The studio produces about twenty films a year. Many of the movies concern the struggle against Japan during the occupation and the ongoing conflict with the United States. Other films tell the story of family life or deal with the everyday concerns of workers and farmers. Historic films are also popular. Few North Korean films are shown outside the country. One film that was shown elsewhere is a North Korean version of a Japanese Godzilla monster movie.

The Pyongyang Film Studios have even made a twenty-four-part historical series for South Korean television. Kim Jong Il takes a great deal of interest in the film studio and is said to have visited it more than six hundred times. Before he became premier of North Korea, he even directed a few films.

The Jikji printing plates seen here are the oldest evidence of movable metal type printing in the world. The plates were used to print books in Cheongju, Korea, in 1377.

Korea's early literature was written using Chinese characters. Histories were among the first works produced. During the Koryo dynasty, two accounts of the Three Kingdoms period were written. The most important history of the Choson dynasty is the *Choson Wangjo Sillok*. This history also includes an encyclopedia with sections on agriculture, the economy, music, geography, and many other subjects.

Korea has many traditional forms of poetry. The longest-lasting style is called *sijo*. This form of poetry has three lines with about fifteen syllables per line. Sijo are personal poems about feelings such as love, grief, or anger. Some sijo, however, have political or satirical themes. Throughout history, women have been more likely to write love sijo, while men have written political sijo.

After the choson muncha alphabet was invented, some Korean writers began using it instead of Chinese characters. Heo Kyun (1569–1618) wrote the first novel in choson muncha, *The Story of Hong Kiltong*. It concerns a man who sets up a classless society on an island without nobles and their laws. Noblewomen in the Korean court also wrote books using choson muncha. The most famous of these is *The Memoirs of*

Lady Hyegyeong, which was written by Princess Hyegyeong (1735–1815). It tells the true story of how her father-in-law, the king, killed her husband, his own son.

Modern literature in North Korea is heavily censored. Some novels tell the story of families or the lives of workers. Others revolve around heroes from Korea's early history or glorify more current heroes who have fought for North Korea, especially Kim Il Sung. Kim himself is credited with writing thousands of books. His name is on the spine and cover, but most were written by unknown authors who received no credit.

A shopper in Kaesong looks at a book by Kim Jong Il.

The most famous sport to begin in Korea is a martial art called taekwondo. North Koreans trace taekwondo to the beginning of Korean civilization, but many argue that its current form is based on karate. At one time, taekwondo was part of Korea's national defense system. Before becoming a soldier, Korean men had to be skilled in taekwondo. Today, taekwondo is still used to discipline the mind, body, and spirit. People all over the world now practice taekwondo, and it became an Olympic sport in 2000.

A North Korean taekwondo expert breaks a wooden board. Taekwondo involves many kicks, jumps, and spins.

Ssireum, or Korean wrestling, is another sport that began in Korea. It can be traced back to about 37 B.C. Ssireum started as a competition among villagers. Two wrestlers wearing cloth sashes enter a ring filled with sand. They grab each other's sash, and each tries to push the other out of ring. Ssireum competitions still take place in small towns and villages during festivals. Archery is also a traditional Korean sport.

Kim Kum Chol (in blue) competes in the World Wrestling Championship. North Korea has produced many successful wrestlers.

Volleyball is one of the many sports enjoyed by North Koreans.

Today, soccer is one of the most popular sports in North Korea. The country supports both men's and women's national soccer teams, which compete in international competitions.

The North Korean government encourages its citizens to take part in sports. In recent years, more North Koreans who have the time are including sports in their lives.

North Korea at the Olympics

The two Koreas have sent separate teams to the Olympic Games since 1948. When South Korea hosted the Olympics in 1988, North Korea boycotted them, so North Korean athletes could not take part. In the 2000 Summer Games in Sydney, Australia, however, the two teams marched together in the opening ceremonies. They carried a banner displaying an image of the Korean Peninsula.

Since 1972, North Korea's athletes have brought home nine gold, twelve silver, and seventeen bronze medals. They have done best in boxing, weightlifting, judo, and wrestling (below).

One of North Korea's greatest Olympic athletes is Kye Sun Hui. In 1996, at age seventeen, she became the youngest person to win an Olympic gold medal in judo. She also won medals at the 2000 and 2004 Olympics.

Daily Life

N ORTH KOREAN MEN AND WOMEN WORK LONG HOURS on farms, in factories, in offices, and at home. Their children study hard in school and after school. North Koreans young and old also find time to get together with family and friends.

Opposite: **About 23 percent of North Koreans are less than fifteen years old.**

North Korean children are required to go to school from ages five to sixteen.

The family holds a special place in the life of North Koreans. Three of the five Confucian relationships deal with respect within the family: children for parents, wives for husbands, and juniors for elders. Parents and grandparents treasure their children. Children treat their parents and grandparents with respect and take care of them in their old age. Younger brothers and sisters also respect their older brothers and sisters.

In the past, a Korean household was made up of three generations. This included grandparents, parents, children, and even aunts and uncles. Although some North Korean

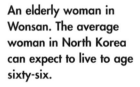

An elderly woman in Wonsan. The average woman in North Korea can expect to live to age sixty-six.

Kindergartners eating lunch. North Korean families have an average of two children.

households still include grandparents, most North Korean households today have only two generations: parents and their children.

North Korean leaders believe that the country's population is too small, so couples are encouraged to have large families. Most couples hope to have at least one son, but families that only have daughters are becoming more acceptable. Because both mothers and fathers work outside the home in North Korea, children are taken care of in nurseries and daycare centers.

In Pyongyang, many couples visit the monumental statue of Kim Il Sung after their wedding.

Time to Relax

North Korean families try to make the most of their time together. Sunday is a day of rest in North Korea. Schools and businesses are closed. On Sundays and special holidays, families go on walks, play in parks, or go fishing. Many who live near a beach enjoy swimming in the summer. North Koreans also maintain close contact with other family members, such as grandparents and aunts and uncles. Important family occasions include weddings, birthdays, and New Year's festivals.

North Koreans are not free to move about the country. A person who wishes to visit a friend in another town must first get permission and a pass to travel. The person then takes a train that might only go 10 to 20 miles (16 to 32 km) per hour. Only high-ranking officials have cars. On the train and in the friend's town, the visitor must show the travel pass to the correct officials. The North Korean government wants to know where people are at all times.

North Koreans line up at a bus station in Pyongyang.

Korean foods have great variety, strong flavors, and hot spices. The national dish, *kimchi*, consists of extremely spicy pickled vegetables. In the past, kimchi and slightly sticky white rice were served at every meal. These days, North Korea suffers from a food shortage. Rice is in short supply, so North Koreans instead use foods made of cornmeal or wheat as their main dish. Kimchi is served when it is available.

The government rations food to make sure that everyone receives a certain amount each month. Important government officials and Korean Workers' Party members receive the

Kimchi

Kimchi is the Korean national dish. The first written description of making kimchi dates to about È·È 1250. If it is available, kimchi is served every day at every meal. Basically, kimchi is pickled vegetables seasoned with red peppers. Vegetables used include Chinese cabbage, cucumbers, or radish roots. Onions, carrots, seaweed, garlic, and pine nuts are other ingredients in kimchi. There are about 170 varieties of kimchi, which is also used as a fiery seasoning in soups and stews. In the past, families made large crocks of kimchi, which they stored outdoors during the winter. Today, some families still make their own kimchi.

most rations. Political prisoners get the least. Many people in North Korea eat only one or two meals a day.

In most North Korean homes, meals are served on a low table with everyone sitting on the floor. In some homes, however, North Koreans sit on chairs at a higher table.

Traditionally, each person had his or her own bowls of rice and soup. Bowls with side dishes of vegetables, meat, and fish were arranged in the center of the table, along with bowls of kimchi and sauces. People would pick up food from these bowls with their chopsticks. They would then dip the food into a bowl of sauce or pick up some kimchi for seasoning. Today in North Korea, meals like this are eaten only in the homes of high-ranking officials. Ordinary North Korean families feel lucky to have one chicken and a few eggs a month.

Traditional Korean meals consist of many small dishes, but in North Korea today, only the elite eat this way.

Pyongyang is filled with large apartment buildings.

Home Life

Until the 1950s, most Koreans lived in houses. They were made with wood beams, clay walls, and thatch roofs. The homes of the wealthy had tile roofs. Rooms were separated by sliding doors made of mulberry paper. The most remarkable part of traditional housing was the heating system, called *ondol*. Channels under the floor carried hot air from the kitchen fire to other rooms in the house. Because the floors were warm, people sat on them to eat. At night, they pulled out mats to sleep on the floor.

Some cities such as Pyongyang have gated areas where high-ranking officials live in private homes. But most North Koreans, even those in rural areas, live in large apartment buildings provided by the government.

In most homes throughout the country, utilities—heat, water, and electricity—are undependable. Because of fuel shortages, most homes have no heat during North Korea's frigid winters. Families bundle up in blankets to keep warm. Water is often shut off for several hours each day. When it's on, the mother or grandmother of the family fills up the bathtub and pots and kettles so there will enough water for drinking, cooking, and cleaning. During the day, the lights sometimes dim. Most evenings, the electricity goes out completely, leaving whole cities in the dark. Then, families light candles. Visitors to Pyongyang have remarked that the only lights on at night are in hotels that cater to foreign visitors.

Everyday Clothing

In North Korea, people wear Western-style clothing to work and to school and, most of the time, around the house. Jeans, however, are not allowed, and women's skirts must cover their knees.

Clothing for Special Occasions

Colorful traditional clothing called *choson ot* is worn on holidays and for special family occasions. Parts of this costume date back to the 600s. The woman's choson ot has a long, full, wrap-around skirt (*chima*) and a short jacket or blouse (*chogori*) tied with a bow to one side.

The man's choson ot has a short jacket (*chogori*) and baggy pants (*baji*) that tie at the ankles. Both men and women wear a long, full coat (*durumagi*) over their outfits. They wear colorful shoes with turned-up toes as part of the choson ot. Because the choson ot has no pockets, men and women also carry drawstring purses (*chumeoni*). These days, few men wear the choson ot, even for special occasions. Instead, they wear a suit and tie.

National Holidays in North Korea

New Year's Day	January 1
Seollal	January or February
Kim Jong Il's Birthday	February 16–17
International Women's Day	March 8
Kim Il Sung's Birthday	April 15
Foundation of the People's Army	April 25
Surinal (Spring Festival)	April, May, or June
International Worker's Day	May 1
Victory Day	July 27
Liberation Day	August 15
Independence Day	September 9
Hangawi	September or October
National Foundation Day	October 3
Korean Workers' Party Founding Day	October 10
Constitution Day	December 27

Holidays and Festivals

Between national holidays and traditional festivals, North Koreans have something to celebrate almost every month. Of the traditional holidays, Seollal and Hangawi receive the most attention.

Seollal, the Lunar New Year, is the first big celebration of the year. This holiday lasts for several days at the end of January or beginning of February. On this holiday, North Koreans perform special ceremonies to respect their ancestors. On the first day of Seollal, some North Koreans wear choson ot. That morning, North Korean families go to the graves of their ancestors. They leave special foods at the graves in a ceremony called *charye*.

Kim Jong Il's birthday is a national holiday. Here, synchronized swimmers perform as part of the celebration.

In the fall, North Koreans celebrate a harvest festival called Hangawi. During Hangawi, people give thanks for the good harvest. The night before Hangawi begins, women in choson ot perform a special circle dance called *kanggangsullae*. In the morning, families again visit their ancestors' graves to leave a food offering and to clean the area around them. Later, they play traditional games and sports, such as turtle tag, tug-of-war, archery, and wrestling.

North Korea's national holidays revolve around important events in the country's history. These include Liberation Day, Independence Day, and Korean Workers' Party Founding Day. The most important national holidays are the birthdays of Kim Il Sung and Kim Jong Il. All these holidays are marked with large parades throughout the country. The largest parades are held in Pyongyang. High-ranking officials watch from a viewing area above Kim Il Sung Square. Usually, Kim Jong Il attends these events for only a few minutes, surrounded by several layers of security guards.

Everyone gets the day off from school or work for these holidays. They get two days off to honor each of the Kims' birthdays. That way, thousands of people can cheer at the parades. Many more watch them at home on television. In the evenings after the parades, young people fill the squares in Pyongyang to dance under torchlight.

North Korea has a rich history and strong culture. Over the centuries, its people have weathered many invading forces and survived with their cultural identity intact. North Korea's current system of government is the most recent challenge they have faced. Hopefully, North Korea will move toward greater openness in the coming years, allowing its people to flourish.

North Koreans dance in Pyongyang on Kim Jong Il's birthday.

Timeline

<table>
<tr><td colspan="2">

North Korean History

</td><td colspan="2">

World History

</td></tr>
<tr>
<td>People are living on the Korean Peninsula.</td>
<td>**ca.** **28,000** B.C.</td>
<td></td>
<td></td>
</tr>
<tr>
<td>The ancestors of Koreans move to the Korean Peninsula from central Asia.</td>
<td>ca. 3000 B.C.</td>
<td></td>
<td></td>
</tr>
<tr>
<td></td>
<td></td>
<td>2500 B.C.</td>
<td>Egyptians build the pyramids and the Sphinx in Giza.</td>
</tr>
<tr>
<td>According to legend, Tangun founds Ancient Choson.</td>
<td>2333 B.C.</td>
<td></td>
<td></td>
</tr>
<tr>
<td></td>
<td></td>
<td>563 B.C.</td>
<td>The Buddha is born in India.</td>
</tr>
<tr>
<td>China conquers the northern part of the Korean Peninsula.</td>
<td>108 B.C.</td>
<td></td>
<td></td>
</tr>
<tr>
<td>The kingdoms of Koguryo, Silla, and Paekche are formed.</td>
<td>ca. 57 B.C.</td>
<td></td>
<td></td>
</tr>
<tr>
<td>The Koguryo Kingdom adopts Buddhism; a Confucian school is founded in Koguryo.</td>
<td>A.D. 300s</td>
<td>A.D. 313</td>
<td>The Roman emperor Constantine legalizes Christianity.</td>
</tr>
<tr>
<td></td>
<td></td>
<td>610</td>
<td>The Prophet Muhammad begins preaching a new religion called Islam.</td>
</tr>
<tr>
<td>Much of the Korean Peninsula is unified under the Silla Kingdom.</td>
<td>668</td>
<td></td>
<td></td>
</tr>
<tr>
<td>Wang Kon, founder of the Koryo dynasty, unites the peninsula.</td>
<td>935</td>
<td></td>
<td></td>
</tr>
<tr>
<td></td>
<td></td>
<td>1054</td>
<td>The Eastern (Orthodox) and Western (Roman Catholic) Churches break apart.</td>
</tr>
<tr>
<td></td>
<td></td>
<td>1095</td>
<td>The Crusades begin.</td>
</tr>
<tr>
<td></td>
<td></td>
<td>1215</td>
<td>King John seals the Magna Carta.</td>
</tr>
<tr>
<td></td>
<td></td>
<td>1300s</td>
<td>The Renaissance begins in Italy.</td>
</tr>
<tr>
<td>The Mongols invade the Korean Peninsula.</td>
<td>1231</td>
<td>1347</td>
<td>The plague sweeps through Europe.</td>
</tr>
<tr>
<td>Yi Song-gye, founder of the Choson dynasty, takes power on the Korean Peninsula.</td>
<td>1392</td>
<td>1453</td>
<td>Ottoman Turks capture Constantinople, conquering the Byzantine Empire.</td>
</tr>
<tr>
<td>The choson muncha (hangeul) alphabet is invented.</td>
<td>1446</td>
<td>1492</td>
<td>Columbus arrives in North America.</td>
</tr>
<tr>
<td></td>
<td></td>
<td>1500s</td>
<td>Reformers break away from the Catholic Church, and Protestantism is born.</td>
</tr>
<tr>
<td>The Manchus invade Korea.</td>
<td>1600s</td>
<td></td>
<td></td>
</tr>
</table>

North Korean History

Japan forces Korea open to trade.	1876
Japan annexes Korea as a colony.	1910
Korea is divided at the end of World War II.	1945
The Democratic People's Republic of Korea is formed in North Korea with Kim Il Sung as premier.	1948
North Korea invades South Korea.	1950
The Korean War ends.	1953
North Koreans attempt to assassinate South Korean president Park Chung Hee.	1968
Famine kills hundreds of thousands of North Koreans.	Mid-1990s
Kim Il Sung dies.	1994
Kim Jong Il officially becomes premier of North Korea.	1997
Leaders of North Korea and South Korea meet for the first time.	2000
North Korea conducts an underground nuclear weapons test.	2006
North Korea agrees to shut down its nuclear facilities; leaders of North Korea and South Korea hold a summit.	2007

World History

1776	The U.S. Declaration of Independence is signed.
1789	The French Revolution begins.
1865	The American Civil War ends.
1879	The first practical light bulb is invented.
1914	World War I begins.
1917	The Bolshevik Revolution brings communism to Russia.
1929	A worldwide economic depression begins.
1939	World War II begins.
1945	World War II ends.
1957	The Vietnam War begins.
1969	Humans land on the Moon.
1975	The Vietnam War ends.
1989	The Berlin Wall is torn down as communism crumbles in Eastern Europe.
1991	The Soviet Union breaks into separate states.
2001	Terrorists attack the World Trade Center in New York City and the Pentagon in Washington, D.C.

Fast Facts

Official name: Democratic People's Republic of Korea

Capital: Pyongyang

Official language: Korean

Pyongyang

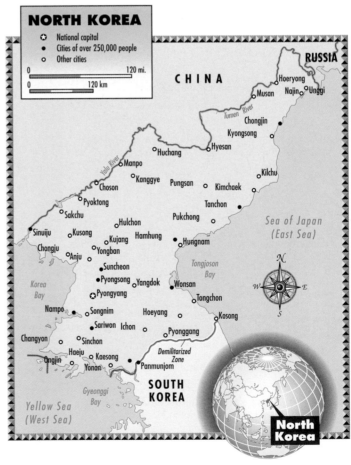

North Korea's flag

Demilitarized Zone

Official religion:	None
Year of founding:	1948
National anthem:	"A Chi Mun bin Na Ra I Gang San" ("Shine Bright, O Dawn, on This Land So Fair")
Type of government:	Communist one-man dictatorship
Chief of state:	Chairman of the National Defense Commission
Head of government:	Premier
Area and dimensions:	46,609 square miles (120,717 sq km)
Greatest distance east to west:	320 miles (515 km)
Greatest distance north to south:	370 miles (595 km)
Latitude and longitude of geographic center:	40° N, 127° E
Land and water borders:	China and Russia to the north; the Sea of Japan to the east; the Yellow Sea to the west; the Demilitarized Zone to the south, with South Korea beyond it
Highest elevation:	9,003 feet (2,744 m) above sea level, Mount Paektu
Lowest elevation:	Sea level, along the coast
Average temperatures:	In Pyongyang, 18°F (–8°C) in January and 75°F (24°C) in July
Average annual precipitation:	40 inches (100 cm)

Mount Kumgang

Currency

**National population
(2007 est.):** 23,301,725

**Population of
largest cities:**

Pyongyang (1999)	3,136,000
Nampo (1993)	731,448
Hamhung (1993)	709,000
Chongjin (1993)	582,480
Kaesong (1993)	334,433

Famous landmarks: ▶*International Friendship Exhibition*,
Mount Myohyang

▶*Koguryo Tombs Complex*, Pyongyang

▶*Kumgang Mountains*, southeastern North Korea

▶*Mount Paektu*, northern North Korea

▶*Tower of the Juche Idea*, Pyongyang

Industry: North Korea's main employers are the government
and the military. Leading manufacturing industries
include cement, chemicals, iron and steel, and
heavy machinery and metals production. Coal,
graphite, iron ore, and lead are the leading
mining products.

Official currency: The won. In 2007, US$1 equaled 142 won.

**System of weights
and measures:** Metric and traditional systems

Literacy rate: 99%

Dancers

Kim Il Sung

Common Korean words and phrases:

Annyunghasimnikka	Hello
Annyeonghigaseyo	Good-bye
Cheonmaneyo.	You're welcome.
Gamsahamnida	Thank you
Ye	Yes
Aniyo	No
Eolma imnikka?	How much does it cost?

Famous North Koreans:

Kim Il Sung (1912–1994)
First premier

Kim Jong Il (1942–)
Second premier

Kim Jong Suk (1917–1949)
Wife of Kim Il Sung and mother of Kim Jong Il

Kye Sun Hui (1979–)
Olympic judo champion

Sejong (1397–1450)
King who encouraged the development of the choson muncha alphabet.

Yi Sun-sin (1545–1598)
Admiral and inventor of the world's first ironclad ship

To Find Out More

Books

▶ Behnke, Alison. *North Korea in Pictures*. Minneapolis: Lerner Publications, 2005.

▶ Dudley, William (ed.). *North and South Korea*. San Diego: Greenhaven Press, 2003.

▶ Goldstein, Donald M., and Harry J. Maihafer. *The Korean War: The Story and Photographs*. Washington, DC: Brassey's, 2000.

▶ Kang, Hyok. *This Is Paradise! My North Korean Childhood*. Translated by Shaun Whiteside. London: Little, Brown, 2004.

▶ Kim, Hyun Hee. *The Tears of My Soul*. New York: William Morrow and Company, 1993.

▶ Koestler-Grack, Rachel A. *Kim Il Sung and Kim Jong Il*. Philadelphia: Chelsea House Publishers, 2003.

▶ Miller, Debra A. *North Korea*. San Diego: Greenhaven Press, 2004.

▶ Park, Frances, and Ginger Park. *My Freedom Trip: A Child's Escape from North Korea*. Honesdale, PA: Boyds Mills Press, 1998.

Video

▶ *Inside North Korea*. Washington, DC; National Geographic Television and Film, 2007.
Journalist Lisa Ling goes undercover into North Korea as part of a medical team and meets ordinary North Koreans. Includes interviews with a former DMZ guard and a former concentration camp guard.

▶ *North Korea: Inside the Shadows*. New York: ABC News, 2006.
TV journalist Diane Sawyer takes a camera crew into North Korea and talks to ordinary North Koreans.

▶ *Nuclear Nightmare: Understanding North Korea*. Silver Springs, MD: Discovery Channel, 2003. Traces North Korea's history and its development of nuclear power.

▶ *A State of Mind*. New York: Kino International Corp., 2004. Follows two North Korean middle-school girls and their families for a year as the girls prepare for the 2003 Mass Games.

Web Sites

▶ **Democratic People's Republic of Korea**
www.korea-dpr.com
The official Web site of the government of North Korea, with information on trade and travel.

▶ **Korean Central News Agency**
www.kcna.co.jp/index-e.htm
The Web site of the state-run news agency of the Democratic People's Republic of Korea.

▶ **North Korea Zone**
www.nkzone.org
For many links and discussions of current news concerning North Korea.

Organizations and Embassies

▶ **Permanent Representative of the Democratic People's Republic of Korea to the United Nations**
820 Second Avenue
New York, NY 10017
212-972-3105

Index

Page numbers in *italics* indicate illustrations.

Japanese language, 47

jing (musical instrument), 104

Jongbaek Church, 97

juche (philosophy of self-reliance), 16–17, 53, 65, 76–77, 84, 85

juche calendar, 53

judicial branch of government, 60

K

Kaesong, 23, 24, *37*, 40, 42, *53*, 71, 73, 76, 81, 88

Kaesong Industrial Region, 23

kanggangsullae (circle dance), 126

Kangnam mountain range, 20

Kim Il Sung, 10, *10*, 12, 16, *16*, 20, 30, 31, 47, 49, 50, 51, 52, *52*, 53, *53*, 54, 55, 58, 59, 61, 62, *62*, 64, 67, 70, *70*, 85, 89, *89*, 96, 98, 105, 109, *118*, 126

Kim Il Sung Constitution, 16, 64, 89

Kim Il Sung Square, 8, 67, 126

Kim Il Sung University, 86

Kim Jong Il, 10, 12–13, *13*, 16, 30, 52, 55, 56, 60, 61, *61*, 64, 65, *65*, 85, 89, *89*, 105, 107, *109*, 126–127, *126*, *127*

Kim Jong Suk, 52, 61

Kim Kum Chol, *111*

Kimchaek, 22

kimchi (national dish), 120, *120*

kimilsungia orchids, 30

kimjongilia begonia, 30

kkwaenggwari (musical instrument), 104

Koguryo Kingdom, 38, *40*, 66, 107

Koguryo Tombs Complex, 107, *107*

Kojo, *51*

Kongmin (Koryo king), 23

Korea Strait, 43

Korean language, 15, 35, 42, 47, 82–83, *82*, 85, 90

Korean Peninsula, 11, 19, 35, 38, 39, 49, 50

Korean People's Army, 65

Korean Revolution Museum, 67, *67*

Korean War, 11, 12, 33, 49, *50*, 51, *51*, 52, 53, 91

Korean Workers' Party (KWP), 59, 63, 120–121

Koreatown, *81*

Koryo dynasty, 23, 40, 41, *41*, 95, 108

Koryo Museum, 23

Kumgang Mountain, 75, *75*

Kumsusan Memorial Palace, 62, *62*

Kye Sun Hui, 113, *113*

Kyongju, 38

L

Lake Cheonji, 28

languages
  accent marks, 83
  apostrophes, 83
  Chinese, 37, 82, 84
  choson muncha alphabet, 82, *82*, 83, 84, *84*, 108
  dialects, 83
  English, 85
  Japanese, 47
  Korean, 15, 35, 42, 47, 82–83, *82*, 85, 90
  Laozi, 92, *92*

legislative branch of government, 60

literature, 108–109, *109*

Los Angeles, California, 80, 81

Lunar New Year, 125

M

magnolia (national flower), 31, *31*

Manchu people, 44

Manchuria, 15

Mangyongdae, 52, 70

Mangyongdae Children's Palace, *101*, 102, *102*

manufacturing, 23, 42, 48, 72, 73–74, *74*

maps. *See also* historical maps.
  geopolitical, *12*
  population density, 80
  resources, *73*
  topographical, *21*

marine life, 22, 33, 71–72

martial arts, 110, *110*

Mass Games, 9–11, *9*, *10*

The Memoirs of Lady Hyegyeong (Princess Hyegyeong), 109

metric system, 75

military, 42, 52, 53, 58, 60, 61, 65, *65*

Ming dynasty (China), 43, 44

mining, 23, 51, 72

missionaries, 45, 90

monasteries, 27

Mongolia, 15

Mongols, 40–41

monsoons, 25

Mount Kumgang, 20, *20*, 27, 28

Mount Kumgang National Park, 27

Mount Kumgang temple, 96, *96*

Mount Kwanmo, 20

Mount Myohyang, 20, 28, 75

Mount Myohyang National Park, 28, 75

Mount Paektu, *14*, 21, 28, 31, 32, 33, 36, 61, 75

Mount Paektu Biosphere Reserve, 28

Mount Puksubaek, 20

mountains, 14–15, *14*, *19*, 20–21, *20*, 28, 31, 32, 33, 36, 61, 75, 80

mudfish, 72

music, 15, 102, 103–105, *104*

Myohyang Range, 20

N

Nampo, 23, 24, 68, 75, 81

national anthem, 64

National Defense Commission, 60

national flag, 59, *59*

national flower, 31, *31*

Meet the Author

PATRICIA K. KUMMER writes and edits educational materials and nonfiction books for children and young adults from her home office in Lisle, Illinois. She earned a bachelor of arts degree in history from the College of St. Catherine in St. Paul, Minnesota, and a master of arts degree in history from Marquette University in Milwaukee, Wisconsin. Before starting her career in publishing, she taught social studies at the junior high/middle school level.

Since then, Kummer has written about American, African, Asian, and European history for textbook publishers. She has also written and edited books about countries, U.S. states, and natural wonders of the world. Her books include *Côte d'Ivoire*, *Ukraine*, *Tibet*, *Singapore*, *Cameroon*, *Syria*, *Jordan*, and *South Korea* in the Children's Press series Enchantment of the World. She also wrote *The Calendar*, *Currency*, and *The Telephone* in the Franklin Watts series Inventions That Shaped the World.

"Writing books about states and countries requires a great deal of research," she says. "To me, researching is the most fun part of a project. My method of research begins by going online. For this book, I found several Web sites and also went to nearby libraries for the most recent books on North Korea. To keep up with events in North Korea, I located Web sites that had daily news reports. Because North Korea's government limits information about the country, it was difficult obtaining accurate, up-to-date statistics and a clear idea about the daily life of its citizens."

Kummer hopes that this book will help young people better understand the history of the Korean people and the current circumstances under which North Koreans are forced to live.

Photo Credits